# A Quiver Full

# A Quiver Full

## Memoirs of a Family Man

Roger Bevan

Greenbank Press

Published by
Greenbank Press
Greenbank
East Horrington
Wells
Somerset BA5 3DR

**British Library Cataloguing in Publication Data**
A catalogue record for this book is available from the British Library.

ISBN 0 9523699 2 3

Typeset by Create Publishing Services Limited
Printed by Bookcraft (Bath) Limited, Midsomer Norton, Avon

# Contents

To Mollie (1924 - 1992)

*Pray for us*

# Foreword

After Mollie Bevan's inimitable autobiography, *Against All Advice*, it is good to have Roger's complementary version of their 50 years of married life, of their 14 children — indeed a quiver full — and of much more besides.

He has a veritable fund of amusing stories which had me chuckling on almost every page. It is fascinating to have passed in review such a remarkable collection of Anglican clergymen from his early years — a type of society which has largely disappeared — and then a unique account of Downside from the 1950s to the 1980s as seen through the eyes of a laymaster, friendly but not uncritical. Roger has had that rare experience of starting his teaching career as the Head Master of his own school, and then becoming a member of a larger and much older community. So he had learnt early that habit of firm and critical assessment which has never left him, but is tempered by a very nice sense of the ridiculous, which must have been an essential element in his survival of fourteen children, thirty-seven grandchildren and in the frustrations of building up such a superb musical tradition at Downside from what was almost non-existence when he came in 1953.

This book will be essential reading for his many friends and pupils, but it stands in its own right and deserves a wider public for its account of a remarkable family, for tracing the course of an unusual musical career, for its experience of the music and ceremonies of the Church of England and of the Catholic Church in the twentieth century, and for its clear demonstration of a mass of unfashionable beliefs and achievements as reasonable and life-fulfilling. Some might even be persuaded to re-examine their own contemporary prejudices and shibboleths. They will certainly be the gainers for reading this book.

DOM PHILIP JEBB<br>
Downside<br>
July 1995

# *Preface*

A distinguished publisher once told me that it was impossible to persuade anyone to read an autobiography unless the author was either famous, had performed daring deeds or had written such limpid prose that even his dullest achievements could raise the spirits of the reader. I cannot pretend to fall within any of these categories: all I can offer is a life uneventful save for the founding of a family of fourteen children. If I am known at all, it is as the father of John, Mary, Gwen, David, Rachel, Tony, Rupert, Cicely, Joe, Jeremy, Stella, Helen, Dan or Ben.

Nevertheless, if the following pages can present the reader with enough entertainment to while away a train journey from Castle Cary to Paddington, I shall be content.

I would like to thank all those who have helped with the production of this book, notably Miss Pepita Perrett for typing the manuscript, my publisher Richard Hudson for many valuable suggestions, my sons John and Tony for much help and Dom Philip Jebb OSB, Prior of Downside, for so kindly writing a Foreword.

RHB<br>
May 1995

# CHAPTER I

## *Early Days*

Many people can still claim to have been born in 1918, but not many to have remembered something which happened before they were born. My memory is, of course, overlaid by later events, but the main story is clear in my mind. Lying in bed I was wakened by a loud, roaring sound in the distance. I called for Mother and asked what it was. 'Oh, that's only the gun firing in Acton Park. Go to sleep and don't worry.' In fact there was a gun in Acton Park, but the last time it was fired was during the final Zeppelin raid of the Great War, three weeks before my birth.

I was born in East Acton, where my father was vicar of St Dunstan's church. This, a gloomy pseudo-gothic building, was erected in the 1870s to serve the rapidly increasing population of the new suburb. When I was born, the urbanising process was not complete: the Church Passage, a track leading from Perryn Road to St Dunstan's was a narrow country footpath, flanked on one side by Frank's Farm and on the other by the huge vicarage garden. Pigs from the farm were known to invade the church and make a meal of the hassocks. On the other side was Friars' Place Lane and beyond that the wilderness of Old Oak Common, a blasted heath, criss-crossed by railway tracks, foot bridges, nettles and dank pools. For reasons which I do not understand we were often taken there for walks. Our favourite outing, however, was to take the tram up Acton High Street and walk to the District Railway station at Acton Town. Here we were in the depths of the country; there was a duck pond outside the station and a pretty lane where we picked blackberries. Industry, however, was not far away: already Wall's ice cream factory had sprung up at one end of our lane; as boys we used to watch at the gate every morning for the procession of tricycles bound for all parts of London with their invitation to 'stop me and buy one.' A huge Ministry of Pensions block next arose on the Uxbridge Road and, in 1928, the whole village, including Frank's Farm was engulfed; that was the year in which we moved.

Our vicarage was large, cold and damp. My father used to say that it was built on top of a subterranean river; certainly prolonged rain would flood the cellar, from which our cat, Obadiah, had to be rescued. The drawing room had to be abandoned during winter, as it was impossible to heat. The garden, however, was a joy. There was a big central lawn surrounded by a path round which my brother and I would pull toy buses, endlessly ferrying phantom passengers along the round — Hellington, Haban, Woodleaf, Prickingham. Turning out of this was a fair-sized kitchen garden, not served by our buses, but containing a walnut tree; it is there that my father had proposed to my mother. Shortly after his marriage my father caught a boy stealing apples from this kitchen garden; he frog-marched the poor boy to the tool shed, locked him in and persuaded Mother to sit on a chair outside and keep watch while he went to fetch, not the police, but the boy's father. On arrival, the father was ordered to give his son six of the best! Times have certainly changed.

Next to our garden was the church, a red brick building of gloomy aspect both inside and out. We were, of course, taken to Matins on Sundays at eleven. Holy Communion was celebrated, in those days, only at the 'early service', before breakfast, or occasionally after Matins for the old people. My father had an excellent choir, one of the best in West London, and frequently put on a cathedral-type service. I became familiar with much of the Victorian repertoire, Bunnett in F, Smart in F, Tours in C and the Stanford services. Sixteenth century polyphony was not sung widely until the Thirties, by which time the choir had vanished. One of our organists, Mr Laird, was very good to me; he once played a piece which I had composed, elaborating the harmonies, so that it sounded better than it was. He often used to let me sit by him while he practised on the three-manual Hill organ; my consuming ambition after that was to be an organist myself. While watching him I was arrested by the pungent smell which issued from his clothes; it was the familiar aroma of malt and hops; Mr Laird, before practising, would pay a visit to the Goldsmiths' Arms. For many years I associated this smell with organ playing.

My father was not a high churchman; he had neither reserved sacrament nor vestments; but he celebrated from the central position, facing the altar and not from the north end. Before the Oxford Movement had made its final impact on the Church of England, many clergy adopted the north end position for celebrating communion, the celebrant and clerk facing each other across the altar. This was known as the Lion and the Unicorn. My father's position in the centre, as in the Roman Mass, was considered 'advanced' and some old ladies were watching for more signs of Popery. He had one curate, Mr Boustead, who had been a long time in the parish and was much respected. He wore a moustache, in those days a sign of low churchmanship. Nowadays I have seen Catholic priests (of the trendier variety) wearing moustaches, but in the Twenties the wearer was considered to be almost a Methodist. My father did not like this ornament and continually urged Mr Boustead to get rid of it. His requests met with no response until one Christmas morning he came down to breakfast to find on his plate a neat parcel wrapped in tissue paper. On opening it he found the hated moustache; he always said that it was the best present he ever had.

My mother was the perfect vicar's wife, perhaps a little too perfect for the taste of some of the parishioners. She chose the hymns and knew the numbers of all those in the Ancient and Modern. Years before she died she chose the hymns for her funeral and charged me solemnly to see that her instructions were carried out to the last letter. Curiously, I had the last laugh in that affair, because just before the service I discovered that she had used the wrong hymn book; had we taken her at her word we should have sung a hymn for the baptism of those of riper years. My mother dressed the choirboys before the opening procession and re-buked the curates for any mistakes they might have made in the reading of the prayers. She accompanied my father to meetings and on home visits; in fact I suspect that she decided who should be visited. Many years later, when they had a car, it was my mother who drove and when my father became an Archdeacon, accompanied him on all his parish visitations. When asked by a friend how she felt having to hear so many sermons, Mother answered 'No feelings at all, I never listen to them.'

My parents were deeply interested in the politics of religion: their conversation at mealtimes consisted entirely of parish affairs and the Anglican ministry, as put before me, seemed more like a business career than a lifelong commitment to the salvation of souls. God was hardly ever mentioned; His name was pronounced 'Gard' but was usually by-passed by some circumlocution such as 'The Almighty'. Once, when advising me about my future, Father said: 'You must begin as a curate in the suburb of a large town. Then, after three or four years you will move to a larger parish, where you will make yourself useful in everything ordered by your vicar. You will then be rewarded with a living, where your hard work and sound judgement will qualify you for promotion to the post of Dean, Archdeacon or even Bishop.' Nothing about the spiritual life.

Most of my time at this period I spent with my brother, Maurice. He was nearly three years younger than I, which is a big difference at an early age. Our relationship was formal with none of the outward display of affection which I have seen among my own children; but then we had no girls. My mother always said that if she had a girl she would drown it. My father, however, longed for a daughter and when Maurice was born he was disappointed. Consequently he seemed to harbour a sort of grudge against him, while Maurice became my mother's favourite. This might have accounted for the somewhat distant relationship between us. Father was always much nicer to me than to Maurice. This situation was exacerbated by my own treatment of Maurice, in which I maintained my superiority with a heavy hand. 'Let's play churches; I'll be the Bishop and you can be my curate.' Any reluctance on his part to fall in with my schemes was punished by blows. The worst day in the year for me was Maurice's birthday; as he unwrapped each present, my jealous complaints grew ever louder, until my bottom had to be smacked. Maurice never grumbled on my birthday.

In one game, however, we managed to play amicably. From the time of approximately my fifth and Maurice's second year we evolved an imaginary country, which we called Rigland. It began with small woolly animals, which we gradually collected until we had ten each. I was, of course, the King and Maurice the Queen. Everything we did was in some way connected with this game, which became more complicated as the years went by. It faded out when I was about fifteen, but by then we had written a history of Rigland, a geography, a book of stories and a collection of songs, 'Riglish songs for Riglish boys.' We also had our own prayer book for use in our daily services. These took place at first in St Dunstan's Church, where we assembled our twenty animals in the front pew; I played a hymn (in the key of C major) on the organ, while Maurice, dressed in a night shirt, processed down the nave, carrying the processional cross. This went on happily without our parents' knowledge until a pious lady came in to arrange flowers, or perhaps to pray, while we were in full swing. Our services were removed to the vicarage. During the summer holidays, however, we used to spend August at Chiseldon, a village near Swindon, where Father looked after the parish while the vicar was away. We could do what we liked there and our daily service was often honoured by a sermon from a rabbit or monkey, or even an elephant.

Mother was not given to displays of emotion. She had been brought up to believe that to give way to one's feelings was vulgar. Her relationship with us was undemonstrative, and there were times when we felt this keenly. One wet day, when we were on holiday at Margate, Mother was lying on the horsehair sofa, when I had a sudden wish to be close to her; I climbed up with her for a cuddle, but she told me to go away and play. That she loved us was plain from the trouble she took to please us, especially during holidays from boarding school, but outward display of affection was taboo. I suppose that this was typical of Mother's generation: Years later, when her brother died, his wife was distressed at the funeral because a bad cold was causing her eyes to water. She was afraid that everyone would think that she was crying.

Our life at St Dunstan's was protected from the outside world and we seldom met other children until we went away to school. We knew no girls and dismissed them as 'silly'. Of the differences between the sexes we were blissfully ignorant and I remember wildly speculating with Maurice about the length of my grandmother's penis. We did not play organised games and were far too lazy at school to take any interest in cricket or football. Seventy years later I now regret that we missed an important part of our education both physical and social.

Our chief amusement was always music. Both Maurice and I took piano lessons from the age of seven and I had the privilege of receiving my first lessons from Miss Katie Moss, composer of the famous Floral Dance. Incidentally she told me later that she sold the copyright for twenty pounds and received none of the vast profits made by the publishers. Maurice had violin lessons but it was the organ which attracted me; I was told that I should learn the piano first, so that I had no organ lessons until I was fourteen. As for entering the musical profession, nothing was further from my thoughts; I wanted to be a clergyman like my father.

Like many children with musically sensitive ears, I was hopeless at sight reading, but could harmonise anything I knew. An example of this took place when I was about seven: I was in bed one night while a parish dance was being held in the hall near the church. It happened that the band was unable to play the National Anthem at the end; instead of letting it pass, my mother immediately sent a messenger to the vicarage to have me brought down to play it. Fortunately I was too young to have been embarrassed by the snide remarks of the parishioners — and of the band.

There was never any question of our attending the state school in East Acton. Such establishments were not patronised in those days by the likes of us; in any case it is doubtful whether the vicar's sons would have received a hearty welcome from the other pupils. We were taught at home until we were old enough for boarding school.

Religious instruction we received from Mother. On Sunday evenings we would go down to the drawing room for the lessons, which consisted of the Anglican catechism and a large amount of the Old Testament. I suppose we studied the Gospels as well, but I do not remember. I do, however, remember Mother telling me that she had religious instruction from her father, who was Rector of West Grinstead in Sussex. This consisted entirely of Old Testament, so that when she went to stay with her Aunt May and was introduced to the Gospels, she sent a post card back to her Father:

> Dear Father,
> I am having a nice time here. Aunt May is teaching me.
> Did you know that there were four Gospels? They are
> called Matthew, Mark, Luke and John. I wondered if you
> had heard about them.
>          Love from Joyse.

We grew up with a good knowledge of the Bible. It is a pity that the Authorised Version, which, apart from its religious content, is the backbone of English literature, should have vanished so completely from modern life. Today the most obvious quotation from it is met with stares of blank incomprehension.

For French I was sent round to Perryn Road to a French lady, Mlle L'Enteri (if that is how it was spelt). I remember little about the lessons, except that Mademoiselle insisted on a correct accent. I was sent at the end of each lesson to see Madame, her mother, who conversed quite unintelligibly and rewarded me with a sticky sweet. My father gave me Latin lessons in his study.

We began our nursery life with a nanny, no Nanny Smith, alas, for she departed after pinning me to a clean 'nappy'. A governess, Miss Asplin, followed, but not for long: she tried to force some fish down Maurice's throat and he was sick all over her. I really enjoyed her discomfiture. A new governess, Miss Dorothy Bates, reigned in her stead. I was brought down for her inspection dressed in my new velvet suit and in a very bad temper. She was better than Miss Asplin but the hours we spent in her company were not, on the whole, happy ones. She was not very fond of children, especially me, and I had reserved opinions about her. However, she gave me my first lessons in company with Maurice and three other children from the neighbourhood. I think she made a good job of this, for when I finally went away to school, I did not find the work too difficult. The only exception was mathematics: I never could do long division and still cannot; problems simply floored me, but I did know my tables. Simple multiplication, addition and subtraction even today constitute the summit of my achievements in maths. At school I had to have extra tuition and ended by passing the School Certificate maths papers by one mark. That was the end of my studies; I took up German after that.

Unless they were doing parish work, my parents saw little of each other during the day time. Father used to shut himself up in his study for hours on end and we saw him only at meals. I was given to understand that he was writing sermons, but cannot imagine that he needed so much time for that. Perhaps, like Archdeacon Grantly, he had salacious French novels hidden in a secret drawer; I do not know. He did, however, read quantities of thrillers. My mother missed adult company and, when we went to school, asked Dorothy Bates to stay on. And on she stayed until I was nineteen! She eventually married my father's youngest brother, Uncle Rupert, but had a sad life. They had no children, Uncle Rupert was not an easy man and they never had any money.

I sometimes wondered how close my parents were to each other. When many years later I questioned Mother on the subject, she was non-committal. Theirs was certainly not a tempestuous love affair. I do not think that Mother was capable of that. In her youth she would attend the grand balls and parties of the London Season: there she would be led reluctantly through the dances by scions of the nobility; she should have been a popular girl, since she was very pretty with a glorious display of red hair; but she had no conversation; all she was interested in was Church affairs, especially choirboys, a subject which found little response from the peers' sons. If any of them showed amorous signs, Mother would run away to seek the protection of her brother. Doubtless Uncle Hughe was not pleased to have his attention diverted from the girls. I suppose that my father was the first man she met who could converse about her favourite subjects, but by then Mother was twenty-three and firmly on the shelf.

They first met at St Dunstan's vicarage. Father had been appointed Vicar in 1916; his sister, Auntie Cecil (of whom more later) was summoned from Chelsea to look after him and to invite to tea a series of marriageable girls, who would, it was hoped, take her place. Mother was number three on this list, but she rapidly gained a foothold by being the only girl not to be bitten by the dog, Mike. In fact she soon became attached to the animal. Long walks in Kew Gardens followed, doubtless illuminated by ecclesiastical topics, until the proposal in the vicarage garden. They were married by the Bishop of London in St Luke's, Chelsea, my Grandfather's church, on July 17th, 1917.

There is an amusing story about their honeymoon in North Wales: staying at Towyn, in Merioneth, they decided on an outing to Dolgoch, travelling on the narrow-gauge Tal-y-Llyn Railway. There were no springs fitted to the carriages so that one was tipped violently from one side to the other, according to which curve the train was negotiating. No sooner had they left the station than Mother decided that she wanted to relieve herself. There of course was no provision for this on board, so she decided to perform by the door, allowing the stream to run under it while the carriage was lurching to that side. Unfortunately, as one might have expected, the lurch suddenly changed to the opposite direction and the whole compartment was flooded. The porter at Dolgoch put his head in through the door and remarked 'Looks as if there's been an accident in 'ere.'

To revert to my own life: several years before I went away I suffered from attacks of tonsilitis. Eventually, when I was seven, I had such a bad attack that I nearly died; I remember hearing Miss Bates telephoning my parents, who were in Manchester, to come back at once. After I had recovered, it was decided that I should have my tonsils removed. For some reason I was not to go to hospital but have the operation at home. I was carried into the nursery, where I beheld Dr Timmins and his assistant, Dr Bishop, both dressed in white robes and standing by the table, peering at bowls and retorts, which fizzed and bubbled furiously. I was stripped naked and ordered to lie down on the bare table. When I refused, I was forced down by a muscular nurse, while I screamed until I passed out. It put me off operations for the rest of my life.

In 1928 my father was appointed Vicar and Rural Dean of Hammersmith. I was sorry to leave Acton but during that one year housing estates had obliterated the countryside of my youth; Hammersmith was uncompromisingly London. The church, another Victorian pile, was less gloomy and more spacious than St Dunstan's. In those days it towered above the Broadway and adjacent buildings; now it can be seen from the Hammersmith fly-over as you pass by at about the same level as the top of the tower. The choir was adequate but not as good as St Dunstan's and I missed Mr Laird and the organ. No private services for Maurice, me and the animals.

The vicarage, ten minutes walk away, was situated on the river bank half way between Hammersmith Bridge and Fuller's brewery, from which fragrant smells wafted into our garden. It was the only private house on the Lower Mall, those on either side having been converted into factories and warehouses. It was an elegant eighteenth century building with three Adam mantelpieces, a spacious drawing room divided by folding doors, and in the cellar the entrance to a smugglers' tunnel. It was blocked up, but I was told that it surfaced in the gentlemen's lavatory in Hammersmith Broadway. The garden was dark and overlooked on all sides; it produced nothing but a few sooty shrubs. Outside the high wall, which separated the garden from the Unwashed, was a network of humble streets, the slums of Waterloo and Marryat Streets. Even at ten years old I was conscious of 'us' and 'them'. This feeling was exacerbated when my mother insisted that, at the age of about thirteen, whenever I went into London I should wear a bowler hat. I dare say that this was normal garb for the children of Belgravia, but in Hammersmith it was a novelty. Dressed in full regalia, I had to run the gauntlet of Marryat Street followed by a crowd of jeering boys until I reached the bus stop. Finally I decided to put the hat into a bag; I do not think that I wore it more than twice. The slums were obliterated in a single night in 1941, when the stone plaque from the Salvation Army hall outside our back gate, inscribed 'Blood and Fire', landed in our garden. Most of the inhabitants, I hope, had been evacuated to the country and their homes now lie buried beneath the M4 motorway. My father spent that night on all fours sheltering beneath his desk.

One advantage of our vicarage was its position by the riverside, half way along the university boat race course. Every spring we would throw a great party to view the race. This party was both clerical and hierarchical: on a sofa by the largest window lay the Bishop of London; the rest of the first floor was reserved for suffragan bishops and arch-deacons; vicars were in the attic, curates on the roof. After the guests had left, Maurice and I helped ourselves to the leavings and ended with a smoke.

# CHAPTER II

❧

# *Relations*

The time was now approaching when I was to go away to school. Before embarking on this phase of my life, I will try to give a picture of some of the relations who coloured my earliest years.

My paternal grandfather as Rector of Chelsea inhabited one of the finest houses in London. It is situated in Church Street, which leads down to Chelsea Old Church, once attended by St Thomas More. Chelsea Rectory was a large eighteenth century house, surrounded by a high wall and enormous garden, in the middle of which stood a mulberry tree. Leading off the drawing room was a spacious conservatory full of exotic plants. Since the Second World War the rectory has become one of the most valuable properties in London and has changed hands rapidly from Arab to Arab. The front door was approached from a gate in the wall, half way down the street and up an imposing flight of steps. It was there that Uncle George, the ninth Viscount Molesworth, and his wife were admitted by Benfield, the parlourmaid, so drunk that they both fell flat on the hall mat. Grandfather was also Archdeacon of Middlesex, so that some comedians in the parish could not refrain from calling them 'The Archdemon and the Horrible Mrs Bevan.' The Molesworths, my grandmother's family, had been pioneers of the Anglo-Catholic movement. One of Granny's sisters, Aunt Andalusia, had married Athelstan Riley, compiler of the English Hymnal. Great Grandfather had been Vicar of Little Petherick, near Padstow in Cornwall; both he and the Rileys are buried in the church in mediaeval style tombs. There was, however, no Anglo-Catholicism about my grandfather. He was staunchly Protestant and had, while Rector of Stoke Newington, sported the dread moustache. He shaved this off when he changed to the more fashionable church of Holy Trinity, Sloane Street. He was at that time what my father called 'a Rising Man'.

Unfortunately he rose no further. For some reason he was eventually moved from one of the principal parishes in London and 'kicked sideways' to the less eminent Chelsea. My father used to say that this was due to his making slighting references to the Bishop during a sermon at St Paul's Cathedral. He was certainly no admirer of Bishop Winnington-Ingram, but I am sure that he would never have been so foolish as to air his views in public. Whatever his faults, Grandfather was very fond of children; when we visited him, he would fling his arms round us and smother us with kisses. This was not an entirely pleasant experience, since he did not stand close to the razor; we used to call it 'falling into a gorse bush'.

Of his own forebears Grandfather never spoke very much. He always said that the first Bevan was called Pip-in-the-Hole, wore no clothes and lived in a cave at Beaumaris, Anglesey. Grandfather's father, Henry Bevan, lived in the Abbey Foregate in Shrewsbury and my father thought that the family had lived there for a long time, having come from South Wales in about 1660. What Henry did for a living was never divulged, but it was said that he had been High Sheriff of the County. His wife, a ferocious woman, was Mary Smalman-Smith, who was a descendant of the Smalmans of Wilderhope Manor on Wenlock Edge. Both Grandfather and his father had been educated at Shrewsbury School, the latter under the great Dr Benjamin Hall Kennedy, author of the famous Latin Primer. There is a story that Henry Bevan was walking through the school with a friend named Bell; the Doctor stopped them and asked their names: 'Bevan, Sir, and Bell.' 'Right' he replied 'Bevan, you go to Heaven, Bell, you to Hell.'

My grandmother, Charlotte, was the second daughter of the eighth Viscount Molesworth. We called her Granny, to distinguish her from my mother's mother, who was Grandmother. We paid fewer visits to Granny than to Grandmother; this was partly, I think, because Mother affected to despise the Molesworths; they were in her estimation rather humble peers and not half so grand as her own family. When visiting Chelsea she was said to put on airs. In spite of this Granny did her best to be kind to Mother, for she was a gentle character when you grew to know her, but slightly uncommunicative and very matter-of-fact: when her second daughter sent her a telegram, announcing that she had decided to become a Catholic, the only reply she received was 'Think you are making a great mistake. Who ordered expensive chicken from Harrod's?'. There is an amusing story which illustrates Granny's imperturbability: a relation named Molesworth St Aubyn suddenly died during tea in the rectory drawing room. Granny immediately rang the bell and everybody waited until Benfield came up from the kitchen

— carrying a fresh plate of bread and butter. She was also highly economical in her life-style; in order to save a penny, she would get off the bus at the World's End in the Fulham Road and walk the rest of the way home. Meals were simple and heating meagre. Nevertheless, Granny was good to us and we grew fond of her when she used to spend a week or two of the summer holidays with us at Chiseldon. She sometimes visited us at Acton, usually just after she had been to see our cousins, Rupert, Mollie and Dick, in Essex. She was always pointing out how superior was their behaviour to ours and no doubt she said the same to them. Consequently, although we never saw our cousins, we were prepared to dislike them without further acquaintance. When we did finally meet at a fête in the Chelsea Rectory garden, my prejudices were confirmed; Mollie was ugly and, worse than that, a girl. Little did I think that twenty years later we should marry and have fourteen children!

One year — I think it must have been 1925 — I was sent away to stay for a few weeks with my Molesworth cousins in Suffolk. The reason was that Mother had been invited to stay with Uncle Hughe and his family at the Beach Hotel in Littlehampton. She was to take Maurice, but I, being liable to wet my bed, would have been *persona non grata*. Accordingly, after showing my dislike of the plan for many days beforehand, I was despatched to Levington where Uncle Charlie ran a farm. He and Aunt Gladys had three children; the eldest, Richard, now Viscount Molesworth, was away at school, but the other two, Jim and Joan, had lessons with a governess and I joined them. I can remember nothing about the lessons, but I suffered agonies from Jim, who was a year older than I, and just big enough to give me a really bad time. After a party at which Jim persuaded his friends to dance round me in a circle, hurling provocative remarks, I decided that this had to stop. One morning, while Jim was absorbed in some game and oblivious of my presence, I crept up behind him and with all my puny strength brought a ping-pong bat down upon his head. To my intense delight he crumpled up and burst into tears. I was afraid that Aunt Gladys would be angry, but she seemed to be quite pleased and even congratulated me on my muscular prowess. I never had any more trouble from Jim. Alas, he died out in the far east during the war. Joan later became a Catholic and died in 1992.

Every year after Easter we would travel to Shropshire, to stay with our grandparents at Quatford Castle near Bridgnorth. Quatford was not a castle in the mediaeval sense, but a folly built in 1830 by a great uncle of Grandfather's, John Smalman, who had also designed the bridge across the Severn at Bridgnorth. It was a beautiful place, a paradise for children. In addition to formal and vegetable areas, the garden was full of mysterious paths and woods. The house itself, faced with red sandstone, was handsome and pleasing to anyone who did not have to pay the bill when lumps of it detached themselves from their moorings. The building was on three levels, from each of which one could step directly into the garden. The rain water collected in a channel on the roof and was sent hurtling down to a series of ponds, all at different levels, until it reached a beautiful rock pool at the bottom of the hill. Drinking water was pumped up from a well, to reach which one had to descend seventy-two steps into the bowels of the earth. That was the job for the gardener's boy; better, perhaps, than with our next door neighbour, Miss Owen of Quatford House; she had a wheel to pump her water; a donkey walked inside it for several hours each day; that was before the days of the RSPCA.

Smalman left the estate to his niece, Mrs Griffith, who in turn willed it to Grandfather when she died in 1889. I do not think that she ever threw anything away, for I remember in the Thirties turning out the drawers of a desk and finding hundreds of letters, some bearing penny black stamps; there was also a small packet labelled 'Uncle Smalman's glass eye.' Some time before the First World War my grandfather suggested that he and my father should explore the 'Dungeon'. This was an eerie cellar which descended from the kitchen and led to a locked door. The key was not found until the day in question. As they edged their way down the steep passage, moisture was pouring down the walls; not the best place for keeping wine. On reaching the bottom they opened the door and there, in front of them, saw what appeared to be a coffin covered with a white pall. Creeping closer they discovered a table so rank with white fungus that it crumbled at a touch. The room was octagonal and full of bottles; a hundred of port, put down in 1840, and other less interesting beverages, including cherry brandy, dating from 1830. No proper brandy though. In such bad conditions it is not surprising that most of the port had turned to vinegar, the corks having rotted away. Four bottles were salvaged, but I was told that they had lost all their quality. I tasted the last cherry brandy on my twenty-first birthday, but it was more like cherryade. The Reverend Edward Griffith, who locked up all that wonderful stuff, must have been a low churchman; I expect he had a very large moustache.

Even the journey to Quatford was an adventure; we took the Kidderminster train from Paddington, which entailed a long wait at Worcester, Shrub Hill. There was a porter there who knew Grandfather and always received a tip of half-a-crown from him. He expected the same from Father and once, when the train stopped, not at the platform, but in the middle, between two other trains, the same porter crawled under the outside train and appeared at our window. We changed at Hartlebury on to the Severn Valley Line with its long-funnelled engine. At Bewdley we would listen for the station master's cry "Arley 'Ighley 'Ampton Loade Eardington Bridgnorth'. Then we would crowd to the window to look for the first glimpse of the white cottages of Quatford on the starboard side. We were met at Bridgnorth by Rutter's car and sped off to our goal. Grandfather and Granny would be waiting for us and we all fell into the gorse bush before tackling Mrs Leary's cakes. Grandfather would take me for walks round the grounds, the Keep Walk, the Bastion, the Curtain Garden, the Croquet Lawn, the Drawing Room Front, the Crescent Garden and the Rock Garden. Meanwhile he used to shower me with compliments, saying how the birds had been awaiting my arrival; this was meat and drink to me at the age of six, but it soon ceased after Granny discovered me giving Maurice a good hiding behind the nursery door. With freedom such as all this provided Maurice and I were really happy. We used to play in an old stable, which housed the family carriage, long since discarded; in an adjoining room was a pile of newspapers dating from Nelson's day. We never, however, held any services, since the church was over a mile away and on Sundays we had to walk there. At Morning Prayer we were fascinated by the Vicar, Mr Pountney Smith, a cousin, who had a loose tooth which waggled all through the service. We expected it to fall out at any minute, but it remained hanging from its precarious roof for years. Mrs Pountney used to entertain us to tea with a mound of egg sandwiches which seemed to reach the ceiling; we had to finish them all and then proceed to a heavy fruit cake. Another diversion at Morning Prayer was the Ancient Briton, an elderly man with a red beard, who used to talk to himself throughout the service and sing tenor in a raucous voice. Out of doors he wore a straw boater, which he used to doff courteously to every lady he met. My grandfather used to say darkly that Mr Britten (for that was his real name) had been a fine scholar, but had come down in the world through drink.

The menu at the castle itself was abundant. In fact I do not know how we managed to eat so much during a day of considerable inactivity. Before food was served there were daily family prayers in the dining room. During my grandparents' time this custom was observed as in most Victorian families. Granny would ring the bell and up trooped the cook (Mrs Leary), Benfield and about three other maids. They arranged themselves along a horsehair sofa, turned round and knelt in a row, so that all we saw were five bottoms which Pixie, the dog, proceeded to inspect. While we were kneeling against our chairs, Grandfather would read a passage from the Bible and a few prayers. Mother, like us, would be kneeling, but she was not praying: she took this opportunity to read her letters. This, I am sure, was just another anti-Molesworth/Bevan ploy. If a Knatchbull had been reading the prayers, she would have behaved herself. Small wonder, then, that when my grandparents died, prayers were discontinued.

We then set to work on the food. On the sideboard would be a hot dish of eggs and bacon, kidneys or kedgeree; there were boiled eggs protected by little woollen caps; on another table was a cold ham or pheasant if in season. The usual toast and marmalade followed. Luncheon at one had three courses. Tea at half past four offered bread and butter, sandwiches and cakes, home-made by Mrs Leary. Then at seven the dressing bell rang in the tower and we all trooped back to change into evening dress and eat a four-course dinner. As small children we naturally did not share all this food, but from preparatory school age until the outbreak of war, that is how we fared. Oddly enough my parents and grandparents did not extend their appreciation of food to that of wine. The only wine my father drank was port, and that not frequently. If visitors came they were offered claret or a white wine, Graves, in those days a somewhat uninteresting semi-sweet wine; I suppose it accompanied the pudding, but I have always been critical of the idea of serving sweet wines with sweet dishes: the food makes the wine taste dry and it loses its character. It is better, I think, to follow the French custom of drinking sweet wines before a meal or at some other time unaccompanied by food.

The Pountneys drove about the village in a pony and trap, but we had no conveyance. If we wanted to go into Bridgnorth we had to walk along the Upper Road, a country lane which went parallel to the main road. The only chance we had of a lift was when we were offered one by Cousin Mary Child, Pountney's sister, who lived in one of Grandfather's cottages in the village. She owned an Austin Seven car, which she drove at considerable danger to herself and the general public. She wore two monocles, one in each eye; when driving along, she would point out some distant view and immediately steer towards it, flicking out a monocle; when she changed direction, the other would be discarded, so that she ended up practically blind. She finished her driving days by crashing into a telegraph pole.

In 1929 Granny, while in London, was discovered to be suffering from cancer. An operation only served to postpone the inevitable. She and Grandfather retired to Quatford, where she died in August 1931. For our holiday that year Maurice and I stayed at another house in the village, inhabited by Ruth Vashon Baker, a great friend of my mother's, and her niece, Pippin. This was the first time we had had a girl to play with and at twelve I found the experience exhilarating. Ruth Baker, unwisely perhaps, decided that Pippin and I should be married. It was quite innocent, of course, for in those days children of our age were ignorant of sex and I thought that boys and girls differed only in the length of their hair. It was an excuse to dress up and have a party. Maurice performed the ceremony, but some of the villagers, especially Cousin Mary, complained to my parents.

Grandfather never recovered from his wife's death. He lived on alone at Quatford, looked after by Benfield and not wanting to see anyone. As the years passed he grew steadily more morose and several times sent well-meaning visitors away in tears. One morning the Vicar of Quatford asked him if he would like Holy Communion to be brought to him; 'No thanks' was the reply, 'I've finished with all that rot.' He died in 1935.

My Grandparents had six children, Hugh (my father), Cecil, Guy, Gwen, Temple and Rupert. Of these there were two who, beside my father, influenced my early life, namely Cecil and Rupert.

Cecil was given a man's name, but I never discovered why; it was her real name, not an abbreviation. Nor did I ever learn why she never married; it was rumoured that she was much sought after in her young days, being rather beautiful, but that all her suitors were killed in the 1914–18 War. Perhaps, however, she froze them off because, although warm-hearted and generous, when displeased she would rear up her chest and head with a slow intake of breath, most formidably. Although she was always ready to play with us children we knew that any bad behaviour on our part would be rewarded with this sign of disapproval.

Cecil, with her younger sister, Gwen, was sent to Dorchester School for Girls, presided over by two spinsters with the improbable name of Kitcat. The Misses Kitcat must have had a great influence over her, because she was for ever quoting their sayings with reverence. On leaving school she became secretary to my grandfather, at the same time qualifying as a religious teacher by gaining the Archbishop's Diploma in Theology (S, Th.). If it had been the fashion then to send girls to the university, she would undoubtedly have distinguished herself for she, unlike my father, was of an academic turn of mind. When my father became Vicar of East Acton, Cecil came to keep house for him and was instrumental in finding him a wife. This done, she took up a post at Macclesfield High School.

Throughout her life Auntie Cecil was a martyr to asthma: she seemed to wheeze all day and was sometimes so bad that she had to stay in bed.

There were no atomisers to relieve her until the late Thirties, when she invested in a cumbersome machine, which she called her 'Puffing Billy'. The only remedy she had before that was asthma papers and she was seen continually crouching and gasping over one of these. I can still smell them. She also, as we learnt later, suffered from multiple sclerosis, which affected her with numbness in her legs. Unsympathetic children that we were, Maurice and I used to stand by her bed, sticking pins with coloured heads through the bed-clothes, while she pretended to cry out in agony. Was she pretending I wonder?

In the late Twenties she went out to Jamaica as Headmistress of St Hilda's Diocesan School for Girls, Browns Town. Here, apparently, her asthma vanished, only to reappear when she came home. This she did every year, bringing us strange, sticky sweets and gigantic shells which, when held to the ear echoed the sounds of Caribbean waves.

In the early Thirties she returned to England in the usual banana boat and settled in a tiny house, 38 Upper Cheyne Row, close to the back gate of Chelsea Rectory. A few doors away stood the Catholic church of the Holy Redeemer and St Thomas More, which was to be so closely associated in later years with the Bevan family.

When the Second World War began Auntie Cecil moved to Quatford to be a companion to my mother. We came then to realise what a good person she was: she had a great sense of humour, was enormously entertaining, and gave a tenth of all her money to charity. In 1944 she took a teaching post in Rugby, where she died suddenly, not of asthma nor multiple sclerosis, but of a cerebral haemorrhage.

Although we loved Auntie Cecil, our favourite was Uncle Rupert, my father's youngest brother. He was nicknamed 'Goggy' originally 'The Mighty Goggy' a title given him at his prep school, where his reputed strength gained him the doubtful privilege of carrying the barrel of water on school picnics. On one occasion he dropped his burden, which then rolled down the cliff into the sea. During the First World War he was commissioned into the Grenadier Guards and was wounded in France. My grandparents were summoned to a Belgian hospital to visit him in what were supposed to be his last days. He told us that when they entered the ward, they spent the whole afternoon talking to the other officers without saying a word to him! He could have gone to Cambridge after the war but decided against it. He was thereupon sent to Malaya to plant rubber. I am told that there are still a few of the older inhabitants of Negri Sembilan who bear a distinct resemblance to Goggy. When he came home on leave, I was warned not to imitate his 'colonial' manners; as these consisted mainly in helping himself to Grandfather's cigarettes, I was not likely to be tempted that way at the age of seven.

During one of his leaves from Malaya, Goggy came down to Eastbourne to take Maurice and me out for the afternoon from school. He arrived in an enormous chauffeur-driven car and drove us into the town. There he called on Miss Hoste, headmistress of a pre-prep school which he had attended in his youth. We were to wait in the car until he came out. We waited for over an hour before there was any sign of him. At last he arrived: 'Right; now for tea; tell me where to go.' I thought hard and settled on The Strawberry Gardens at Wannock, where we had been with our parents. So off we drove. When our destination was drawing near, I nudged Goggy, who was staring out of the window; 'Here we are' I said. 'Bloody rotten place this — not even a pub; let's go on.' So on we went, this time to Beachy Head. There was a pub there. Goggy stopped and went in. After another hour he came out; but it was time to go back to school and we never had our tea.

Some time in the late Twenties he returned home finally, having conceived a strong liking for the whisky bottle. Unable at first to find work, he went to live at Quatford Castle after Granny's death, to keep Grandfather company. This was the worst thing that could have happened. The two had never seen eye to eye; Grandfather shut himself away and would have nothing to do with him. Goggy filled a few hours each week giving lessons to his nephews and niece, Rupert, Mollie and Dick, but the rest were spent at the village pub, The Danery. He had a store of bottles at the Chantry, where his sister, Gwen, and her children lived. When his pupils discovered them, he told them that they were fairy bottles and that their mother was on no account to be told of them.

The situation became so hopeless in the end that Goggy had to be sent to live with us in London. There he found a job with a stock jobber's firm but I fear that he must have been the tea maker, since he knew nothing about finance. My parents had much to suffer over his drink troubles, but he was a wonderful companion to Maurice and me. I do not expect that he enjoyed playing games about Rigland, but he made us think that he did. He would amuse himself for hours sitting at the piano and picking out his favourite hymns, often singing the tenor part so loudly that it could be heard in the garden. The presence of an unmarried female, Dorothy Bates, in the house was more than Goggy could resist and a romantic affair soon blossomed. I do not think he intended ever to marry her, but I do remember my parents looking very serious and calling a family conference. Maurice and I were naturally not invited, but we listened at the key-hole and heard the sound of voices raised in anger and a female (Dorothy?) in tears. After an hour or so a bulletin was issued that Rupert and Dorothy were to be married. The wedding took place at Quatford Church in September 1937; I was nineteen then and was chosen as Goggy's best man; his brothers were all abroad and my father was conducting the ceremony. My cousins, Temple's children, came home from Hong Kong at this time and the youngest of these, Pamela, was bridesmaid. Afterwards, accompanied by Pippin, I drove the newly-weds to Stratford-on-Avon; on the way home, late at night, Pippin put her head on my shoulder. Although nineteen, I was still very green; I thought she was just feeling tired. Damn!!

Poor Dorothy had a miserable time. They had neither children nor money. Shortly after Mollie and I married we met them for drinks at the Savoy Hotel. As we left, Goggy took out his wallet and dealt out a handful of pound notes, for, like most of the poorest in our family, he was touchingly generous. Aunt Dorothy was waiting at the door: 'Please can I have them back? It's all we've got to live on for the next three weeks.'

When War broke out again in 1939 Uncle Rupert was delighted. He was given back his commission in the Brigade and served in administrative posts, being too old for active service. He even spent some time in Australia. It was the happiest time of his life. When peace came, he returned to the old insecurity and was frequently out of both work and money. His old war wound began to bother him and there were bouts of pleurisy. Finally, in about 1960 Rupert and Dorothy retired to my father's new vicarage at Stanton Lacy near Ludlow. There Goggy's health declined fast until he died in the freezing winter weather of January 1963.

My father's other brothers we scarcely knew at the time, since they lived abroad. Uncle Guy was a most successful engineer. As a young man he had installed an engine at Quatford and wired the house for electric light. I always think of the Castle in connection with the humming of that engine. It produced only light. We had to wait for the mains before we could have heating.

From the early Thirties onwards Uncle Guy lived in Canada and eventually rose to be managing director of the famous firm of Massey-Harris, as it then was. Periodically he would return home and his visits were keenly anticipated. He usually arrived with a new car. Grandfather mistrusted cars, but on one visit Uncle Guy brought a magnificent Daimler and offered to take us all, including Grandfather, for a drive. 'Now' said Grandfather 'see that you go no more than twenty-five miles an hour; I can't stand anything faster.' 'All right' answered Uncle Guy, 'twenty-five miles an hour it is.' We set off up the Stourbridge Road. After some time Grandfather remarked 'This is just what I like — twenty-five miles an hour.' I looked at the speedometer: it registered seventy.

Uncle Temple was the youngest but one. He owed his unusual name to Grandfather's admiration for Frederick Temple, Bishop of London and later Archbishop of Canterbury. He was the only male member of Grandfather's family, apart from my father, to produce children. They were Sonia, Michael and Pamela. They lived in Hong Kong for all of my childhood, so that, apart from the brief meeting at Dorothy's wedding, I hardly knew them. In later years, when they settled in England at Longstowe Hall, I became friendly with them all.

Our Tuesday visit to Grandmother Knatchbull-Hugessen, Mother's mother, was a serious occasion. Maurice and I were severely warned against any lapse in good behaviour; in fact we were so polite that for most of the visit we were speechless. A roofless double-decker bus took us from Acton; somewhere along the route we changed from a No 7 to a No 11, which deposited us at Chelsea Barracks. From there it was a short distance to Burton Court, an imposing block of flats, where Grandmother lived on the ground floor. I have in my room an oil painting of her at the age of about twenty-five, where she appears as a beautiful young girl with piled up blonde hair and a seraphic expression. By the time I knew her, age had made its inroads; the seraphic expression had changed to severity and an air of disapproval which I found intimidating. I once dropped and broke a cream jug; at some point in every succeeding meal she would turn her frown on me and remark 'Who broke my cream jug?'

For me the main attraction of the visits to Burton Court was gastronomic: Grandmother always lived well, although she ate little herself. While she sat sipping brandy and water, we were busy tucking into sole, lamb cutlets or peaches and cream. In spite, however, of my addiction to the pleasures of the table, I was extremely thin and a regular bed wetter. One Tuesday I was stripped naked and paraded before the formidable old lady. As she ran her eyes over my skinny body, I was mortified. But worse was to come. My mother was doubtless in quest of a cheque for medical attention. This was presumably forthcoming, for I was duly hauled off to see a Harley Street specialist. His cure for my thinness was welcome: cream for breakfast every day. For bed wetting, however, the remedy was bizarre: each night in the bath I had to have a can of freezing cold water poured over my bottom. When that had no effect, a nightly beating was ordered. Mother had to do this and I remember following her round the garden, while she searched in the shrubbery for a suitable cane. It made no difference; in fact it was not until I reached boarding school that I was cured by the ridicule of the other boys.

Sometimes when we visited Grandmother, Uncle Hughe, my mother's brother, would join us. He was at that time working at the Foreign Office. He would often give us each half a crown, at least until one day, when he telephoned my mother to say that he was unable to come; I asked to speak to him and, before my mother could stop me, shouted 'You can leave the half crown on the hall table.' In my childish ignorance I thought this a good joke; but there was a shocked silence, a brief conversation with Mother and no more half crowns.

Grandmother was one of the six children of Admiral Sir Alexander Montgomery Bt. Of these I knew only three. Aunt Flo' was considered the intellect of the family since she was the author of a number of sentimental novels. One of these 'Misunderstood' was well known and later filmed; years later Uncle Hughe gave me the proceeds of the film rights. When I was a small child, she took a fancy to me and wrote a poem in my honour. Unfortunately I remember her only as a vague figure, dressed in black and sitting in an armchair. She died when I was four. To other members of the family she was not always as pleasant: When Uncle Hughe presented his fiancée, later my Aunt Mary, Aunt Flo' quizzed her through her lorgnettes and asked 'Are you sufficiently educated to marry my nephew?' She and her sisters had, after their father's death, lived with their mother in Cadogan Place. There they dwelt in seclusion like nuns and were not allowed ever to see a man. How my grandmother and her older sister managed to get married passes my comprehension but, as they both married clergymen, perhaps their mother did not consider them to be proper men. Next door lived the Macmillans and their small son Harold, later to be Prime Minister. When my mother was there on a visit she was not allowed to play with the Macmillans because, being publishers, they were considered to be 'in trade'. The Montgomerys were great snobs: when the youngest daughter Ethel died she left instructions that she was to be buried as far as possible from the poor.

One of Mother's tasks as a young girl was to stand at a window overlooking Sloane Street and shout to Lady Montgomery whenever a car drove past. Sadly the old lady never reached the window in time and died without ever seeing a car.

I knew little about the Montgomerys because my mother told me very little about them and I was too young to be interested. My great grandfather, the Admiral, was said to be so absent minded that he used to rise from his chair and stagger about the room bent double. 'Whatever are you doing, Papa?' asked the girls 'Oh, I'm sorry, I forgot to unbend myself.' His brother, Uncle Alfred, had two beautiful daughters, one of whom married the Marquess of Queensberry. It is related that on the wedding night she burst out of the bedroom and ran screaming through the house. However, she must have grown accustomed to her husband's attentions, because in due course she became the mother of Lord Alfred Douglas, the friend of Oscar Wilde.

The most colourful of the Montgomery relations was Mrs Deresse, Cousin Augusta. How she was related to Grandmother I know not, but she was more absent minded than the rest. On one occasion she is said to have descended from a taxi in South Kensington, holding her handbag upside down and open: out poured a cascade of gold sovereigns straight down a drain. I wonder if they are still there or whether some council worker treated himself to a week in Paris. In her old age she became unable to control her wind, so that her conversation was punctuated by explosions, particularly evident at family prayers, when she would read the Bible in a dramatic voice: 'How are the mighty fallen!' Brummm-m-Bang!

To revert to our visits to Burton Court: after lunch we all trooped upstairs to Flat No 8 inhabited by two of Grandmother's sisters, Aunt May and Aunt Mum. 'Mum' was a nickname which she had given herself as a child; her real name was Ethel. We loved Aunt May, who always took the trouble to talk to us as people and not 'kids'. Aunt Mum was less popular, although she could be generous. She disapproved of my mother, always comparing her unfavourably with Uncle Hughe, and we suffered from her reflected displeasure. She had a peculiar way of tipping us: when I went away to school she gave me ten shillings and Maurice only five, because he was still at home. When Maurice went to school I still had ten shillings because I was in the Upper School and Maurice five because he was in the Lower; finally I received ten shillings when I went to Shrewsbury but Maurice five because he was still at prep school; and so it went on; poor Maurice could never catch up. The aunts used quaint expressions and pronunciations which must have dated from the eighteen-fifties: they said 'ain't it' and 'I declare'; the 'h' in 'hotel' was also dropped. My mother also spoke like her mother's generation: 'gorn' for 'gone', 'lorst' for 'lost' and 'larndry' for 'laundry'. The word char-à-banc had to be pronounced in the French way, rather than the plebeian 'charabang'. She considered other pronunciations 'non-U' and we were forbidden to use them.

We would often be sent during the afternoon to play with the servants. I do not know whether they resented having their afternoons disturbed, but they never showed it. We used to spend hours talking to them and playing with their crystal wireless set.

Sometimes Aunt Mum took us all for a shopping expedition in her 'motor'. She was the first person in the family to have one; and more than that, she had a chauffeur as well. His name was Ricks; all upper servants were known by their surnames, lower ones by their Christian names. Ricks would drive us sedately up Sloane Street and park outside Harrods, where we would wait in the car while Mother and Aunt Mum went in to buy various garments. You could park anywhere in those days; there were no traffic lights, one-way streets, yellow lines or even driving tests. At the end of these excitements we travelled home on the open bus again. It always rained; Maurice was sick on the top deck and I wet my trousers.

Of my mother's Knatchbull relations I saw few. Uncle Hughe was soon posted abroad and rose to fame later when, as Ambassador to China, his car was attacked by a Japanese aeroplane. That was in 1936; later still he became Ambassador to Turkey and figured in the 'Cicero' affair. Aunt Mary always maintained that he had been unfairly treated by Ernest Bevin, the Foreign Secretary, and that, were the truth allowed to be known, no blame could be fastened on him. I saw from time to time his three children: Norton had been a delicate child, spending much of his youth in hospital. He was a few years older than I and I sometimes lunched with him when we were at Oxford together, I as an undergraduate and he reading for a D Phil. One day early in 1939 he killed himself by an overdose. The reasons for this were never divulged. Elisabeth married Sir George Young and was the mother of the present Minister. She died of cancer, leaving only Alethea, who is happily still with us.

The generations between my great-grandfather and myself were few in number but spanned many years. It is almost incredible that my great-grandfather, Sir Edward Knatchbull was MP for Kent at the time of the Catholic Emancipation crisis in 1829. He married three times, his second wife being Fanny Catherine Knight, the favourite niece of Jane Austen. Her children, from whom I am descended, assumed the additional surname of Hugessen, after their paternal grandmother. This proved to be such an inconvenient mouthful that my great uncle, Lord Brabourne, dropped it from his side of the family.

Sir Edward's third son was Reginald, my grandfather, who became a clergyman, ending as Rector of West Grinstead in Sussex. He again married twice so that my mother possessed two half-brothers and four half-sisters. Her two real brothers were Uncle Hughe and Uncle Maurice, who was killed in 1916. Sir Edward also had an interesting fourth son, Uncle Herbert, who was MP for Faversham. He was the favourite uncle, unmarried it was presumed, and a welcome visitor to West

Grinstead at Christmas time. 'Poor Uncle Herbert, he must be so lonely. Let's invite him to stay.' In 1917, when my mother married, a strange change overcame Uncle Herbert. He became embarrassed and furtive. Eventually he confessed to Grandmother that for many years he had been living in Shepherd's Bush with an ex-housemaid from some great house where he had once stayed. He had already begotten eight children and was afraid that his Shepherd's Bush domain might be visited by the Vicar, my father. He need not have worried, since Shepherd's Bush was not in my father's parish. Having confessed, Uncle Herbert thought that all would be forgiven, but it was not. Grandmother had staunch ideas about such things and broke off relations, even after he had married his beloved. The whole family professed abhorrence of the affair, but I fancy that my mother secretly admired Uncle Herbert.

There was an amusing sequel to these events. Years afterwards, when Grandmother was moving into Burton Court, she noticed one of the furniture movers gazing at a picture of Sir Edward. 'Yes,' said Grandmother 'it is a very nice picture. It is my father in law.' 'Yes, madam,' answered the furniture mover 'and my grandfather'.

# CHAPTER III

🍃

# *Aldro*

My parents had always intended to send me away to boarding school. My father had been educated at Durnford House, Langton Matravers, Dorset, but although it was considered at the time to be a good school, he was never happy there. There was one particularly barbarous custom of requiring every boy to dive off the Dancing Ledge into the sea. If a boy shrank from the performance, he was liable to be thrown in, a hazardous operation because below the rocky ledge were huge boulders projecting from the foaming waves. My musical proclivities indicated a cathedral choir school, and St George's, Windsor, was suggested. Had they kept to that idea I should have sung under Sir Walford Davies, been given a thorough grounding in music and possibly ended up in a cathedral career. As it was, music was considered throughout my student days to be of secondary importance. My parents finally decided on Aldro School, Eastbourne, run by a son-in-law of the Rector of West Grinstead, my grandfather's successor.

I first went to school in the summer term of 1927. Well do I remember the taxi ride to Victoria Station, growing ever more wobbly at the knees as we approached the huge concourse of boys and girls, some laughing, others tearful, picking our way among piles of trunks and wooden tuck-boxes. Unlike many children today, I loathed going back to school and was never really happy there until I was over sixteen. Most of the boys travelled by train, although many of their parents owned cars and even chauffeurs, but long-distance motoring was unusual. For my first term I travelled earlier with my parents and stayed with Auntie Gwen (Dyson-Laurie), Granny's younger sister, who lived in Staveley Road, Eastbourne. They stayed with her whenever they visited me. I was prepared to be homesick when I said goodbye to them and watched them walking away down Darley Road; strangely enough, though, I was so full of excitement that it was a day or two before I felt the pangs.

We were well taught in spite of the shortcomings of some of the staff. Apart from the Headmaster, Mr F. E. Hill, and two others, none of them were vocational teachers; some were schoolboys waiting to go to university, others were retired army officers, often partially disabled by war wounds, without any teaching experience. This was normal in preparatory schools until recent times. I once taught part-time in a school in which one master had no 'O' levels. In spite of this, I was given a good grounding, especially in Latin, the only language in which teaching methods had not changed for centuries; we were made to learn our grammar and no one ever supposed that we were to consider Latin as a modern language or even to enjoy it. I, as well as some others, enjoyed it because it was taught so logically that we could be conscious of our own progress and were never floundering in a morass of vagueness and uncertainty. It is the consciousness of 'getting somewhere' which kindles a child's interest.

The school, however, never officially cherished high aims for academic success. When my father suggested that I should be coached for a scholarship to Shrewsbury, the idea fell on stony ground. They did not encourage scholarships, he was told, unless boys could take them 'in their stride' — whatever that meant. I had to learn Greek, which they did not offer, and to do this had to sacrifice both English and mathematics. Latin grammar, prose and verses (yes, we wrote those at the age of twelve) gave me all the English I needed, but I never recovered from the loss of maths. My classics teacher for my last two years was a great character, 'Johnny' Walker. He was a little wizened old man, shabbily dressed and very thin. I do not suppose that he could even feed himself properly on the miserable salary which the masters received. He gave us an understanding of the meaning of scholarship and an ambition to excel. We gave him a bad time, in spite of this, even throwing blank cartridges into the coal fire while he was standing in front of it, but we always respected him. Any careless mistakes on our part were rewarded with the well-known rebuke: 'Scholarship in waste paper basket, bi (he always called us 'bi'), you wouldn't even pass into Brixton Grammar School.' I am sure that Brixton Grammar School is a fine school, but Johnny made it sound like the entrance hall to hell.

Scripture was taught by Mr Hill. This, as at home, was Old Testament only, except for the Acts of the Apostles, which were considered to be less sacred than the gospels. Possibly this emphasis on the Old Testament derived from the fact that there was a large number of Jews in the school. We were, however, very carefully taught and I still feel that I know more about Ahab and Jezebel than about those parts of the Bible which are more relevant to the Christian faith.

Very little importance was attached to music and I was considered an oddity to have any interest in it. The chapel singing was entirely unison, both Anglican chants and hymns, except when the second master, Mr Craft who sat at the back, put in a tenor part, always flat. Singing was done on half holidays, half the school at a time, when we ploughed through 'British Songs for British Boys'. Curiously enough, the Head-master's nephew, Peter Burton, was the only outstanding musician in the school; he gained his FRCO Diploma at the age of sixteen and ended as organist and choirmaster of St Alban's Cathedral. He died while rescuing one of his choristers from drowning. Peter, however, was a weekly boarder and had music lessons at Eastbourne College where his father was a housemaster.

It was sometimes possible to pull the wool over Mr Hill's eyes, so unmusical was he. On one occasion I had to do this, to save myself from his displeasure and ridicule. We had just assembled for a scripture class when Mr Hill entered and threw me a magazine which contained a hymn about animals. It must be understood that at that time I could play and harmonise anything I knew, but reading at sight was quite beyond my capabilities. I looked at the hymn, which was in B flat and impossible. I therefore made up a tune of my own. 'That's good, Bevan; play it again.' The remark nearly threw me, since I could not possibly remember what I had played; I therefore produced another tune 'Good,' said Mr Hill 'play it a third time.' Another completely different tune followed, but he was so pleased that I received congratulations and gracious smiles when I passed him in the corridors. He even called me 'archdeacon' which he always did when he was pleased with me. My other musical contributions did not always receive such praise. The chapel boasted a one-manual pipe organ, played by Miss Browne, the singing teacher. It was blown by the boys, who revelled in pumping so hard that the weight would descend to a line marked 'bursting point'. When this was reached, there was no explosion, but an even more entertaining effect: all the notes used to go down together, so that Miss Browne was driven to distraction. My misfortunes began when she fell ill and I had to play in her stead. No one noticed that I played the hymns by ear and in the key of C, but what caused the trouble was my use of a stop called 'Open Diapason'. While the other stops were harmless dulcianas and flutes, this one seemed to be on a particularly high wind pressure. Miss Browne reserved it for the last verse of a triumphalist hymn, or for the National Anthem. I, however, chose to use it to ginger up the Creed. The results were dramatic; everyone stopped singing and

Mr Hill gave me a sour look, which he repeated in the corridors. He stopped calling me 'archdeacon'.

You could not remain for long in Mr Hill's favour if you were not good at games. I was not even interested in them but had to spend hours and hours playing them, especially in the summer term. At football I think I can say that I scored only once and that was an 'own goal'. Rugby football was played only half-heartedly during the Lent term; perhaps the half-heartedness was on my side only, because I only played once, when I was sent off the field for having a theological discussion with my friend, 'Pip' Freeman.

Our life at Aldro was, I think, more Spartan than is usual these days. Except at half term in the Christmas and summer terms, we never saw our parents. It was considered unsettling for us to see them more often. We could not telephone them; trunk calls were expensive and, in any case, there was no instrument available. Throughout the year we had a period of drill before breakfast; sometimes with the whole school together, at others by 'squads', into which the school was divided. These were named after the dominions and colonies of the British Empire, whose grandeur and permanence was continually impressed upon us. The drill classes culminated at the summer half-term in a magnificent display in front of the parents, when the boys, dressed in white flannels and blazers, paraded in their squads, accompanied by the flags of the Empire. Mr Craft gave the orders by whistle. Thank goodness he did not sing. During summer, before drill, we had to jump naked into the 'plunge', an icy cold swimming bath in the gymnasium. This activity was often watched by an audience which included Mrs Hill and her young daughter, Pansy.

The food was often insufficient in both quantity and quality; in fact there were times, especially at lunch, when it was uneatable. The meat was so full of gristle that one could not swallow it. Some of the puddings were revolting, especially a cornflour mould, covered with skin, which we were expected to eat with golden syrup. Tea, or supper really, as it was the last meal, consisted of bread and butter. At least for my first two years we had to supply our own jam or cake but could not have access to it unless the matron put it on the table. If she decided not to do this, I was forced to rely on friends, who were thin on the ground, or else go without. There were times when, the butter being finished, I had to fall back on bread and salt. No wonder that each night, as we paraded with milk and a biscuit to say good-night to Mr Hill, my mouth would water at the sight of the staff supper being wheeled past us on a trolley. A dish of fried plaice really stimulated my gastric juices.

An embarrassing episode once occurred in relation to the jam which we had to supply for our tea. My father was very keen on walking and used to go on tours in the West Country. Once he decided on Sussex, walking from Birling Gap to Eastbourne and ending up at Aldro for tea. He was put, not with me, but at the high table next to a boy called Andrew Hawes. Hawes was fond of Golden Shred marmalade and kindly passed the jar to my father. By the end of the meal the marmalade jar was empty. Hawes was not at all pleased and attacked me afterwards with uncomplimentary remarks on my father's appetite and size. I duly passed on the remarks and a few days later a new pot arrived on Hawes's table.

One Christmas holidays, just before we were due to return to school, Mother took us to Barker's in Kensington to stock up for the term. I had my eye on a repulsive confection made in the shape of a tortoise and covered with green icing. I took it back to school, eagerly awaiting the day when Matron would put it out by my place. Weeks went by, even months, and no tortoise cake appeared. Finally I plucked up courage to ask after it; Matron was plainly irritated by my request but agreed to look in the cupboard. After a long search she discovered, in a far recess, a green slimy mess of putrescence, covered with white fur. I never tasted my tortoise cake. So hungry was I that I thought about food all day, especially Lyons' French cream sponges, which helped my imagination to while away the late afternoon gym classes. Occasionally, though, we had a treat, when some parent would present sausages for tea. At the end of the Christmas term we had a wonderful dinner with turkey and all the extras. This, which was known as 'The Feast', did something to make up for the fast of the previous weeks.

The Victorians considered that *mens sana in corpore sano* could be preserved only by regular evacuation of the bowels each morning after breakfast. This rule was fiercely enforced at Aldro by means of a school list, which was fixed to a wall near the lavatories. After a successful motion each boy was expected to tick off his name. After lunch every day Mr Hill would read out the names of those who had not 'ticked off'. 'I forgot, sir' was punished by a bad mark; 'I couldn't go, sir' meant being immediately despatched to the matron for a dose of syrup of figs. I only hope that too many men who were boys at this time did not die of severe internal complications.

In the end I was sorry to leave Aldro. I had made some friends by then and it was leaving them that caused the wrench. The school was not suitable for me, as my interests were barely catered for. I won the Shrewsbury scholarship but still wish I had been sent to a choir school.

Although most of the five years from 1927 to 1932 were spent at Aldro, some of that time was obviously passed at home on holiday. At

Christmas we were in London, during part of Easter at Quatford and in the late summer months in various other places. London in the Twenties and Thirties was a pleasant place on the whole although there seemed as many cars and lorries as now and they gave forth a louder noise and stronger smell. A pre-war lorry in second gear really screamed at you; then there was the ubiquitous smell of tobacco; nearly all adults smoked and a non-smoking carriage in a train was not easy to find. I do not think that as a child I noticed the tobacco smell, nor would have minded if I had. There were no skyscrapers and it was possible to stand on top of the tower of St Paul's, Hammersmith and see as far as St Paul's Cathedral without anything to block the view. Best of all, provided he watched the traffic, it was quite safe for a boy of my age to travel alone to the West End; this I frequently did after the age of about eleven, finding my own way everywhere on the underground. Fares by present standards were ludicrously cheap. Fourpence from Hammersmith to Piccadilly Circus on the tube; and I once travelled by tram, accompanied this time, from Westminster Bridge through the Kingsway tram tunnel and all the way to Poplar for a penny. For another penny I rode through the Blackwall Tunnel and along the South Bank to Putney Bridge. I often bicycled across Hammersmith Bridge, through Barnes and Roehampton, to Richmond Park and back.

During school holidays Mother always put herself out to see that Maurice and I had a good time. Before Christmas we would visit the bazaars in all the big shops: Harrods, Barkers, Whiteleys, Selfridges, Gamages. After looking at the model trains we would visit whatever speciality was on offer, a ride in a submarine, a flight in an aeroplane or some other imaginary adventure. We always visited the Bertram Mills circus at Olympia — at least the fun fair, which we preferred to the circus itself. Once I felt very guilty at spending £1 at the fun fair; I suppose it was rather a lot, seeing that most of the items cost no more than threepence or sixpence. Then there were the theatres and cinemas. We saw at least one West End play each week in January, matinees of course, which would be followed by tea at Lyons Corner House or Fullers or the Cadena. We went to as few parties as possible, as we both hated them; we certainly never gave any. At Easter we visited the Ideal Home Exhibition at Olympia. I was fascinated by the food stalls which gave away samples. We used to return home laden with miniature loaves of bread, cornflakes packets, Marmite and various jams.

Each August from 1922 to 1932 my father used to take a locum at Chiseldon, a village of thatched cottages four miles from Swindon. We travelled there by a somewhat complicated train journey from Paddington. We had to change at Newbury and Savernake and then walk about half a mile up to the high-level station, which was on the 'Midland and South-Western Joint Railway'; this ran from Andover to Cheltenham and stopped at Chiseldon. Maurice and I found this journey rather boring, especially the walk at Savernake, and we drove our parents mad by asking, every time we passed a wood 'Is this Savernake Forest?'. The porter at Newbury was rather sarcastic about our luggage: 'Here you are again with your dogs, cats, rabbits and parrot.' Although we only had a dog and a cat, we certainly did things properly with the luggage. I remember counting fifteen trunks on the platform one year. The party consisted of ourselves, Dorothy and two maids. For the holiday we left the cook at home and secured the services of Mrs Jones from the village. She was a better cook, who specialised in the most wonderful meringues, of which we, especially Mother, ate an inordinate amount.

The vicarage was an eighteenth century house with a large garden stretching up a hillside. In early August it was burgeoning with fruit. Maurice was fond of gooseberries, which he ate, skins and all, and was thereupon sick all night. We often went out for picnics, sometimes by train to Marlborough, followed by a walk into Savernake Forest; at other times a local trip to Liddington Castle, an iron age earthwork nearby, round which Maurice and I would play trains; we had to walk there, pushing a handcart containing the lunch. How we grumbled! My father usually came with us; he did not enter much into the local village life, except to take services on Sunday and any odd funeral which might crop up. On one occasion the local Squire, Major-General Calley, invited him to come out shooting. What they could have shot in August, I cannot imagine; surely there are no grouse on the Marlborough Downs; perhaps it was rabbits. Anyhow, my father simply replied to the invitation: 'No thanks, I haven't got a pistol.'

The weekly visit, either by train or by the ramshackle Bristol Tramways bus to Swindon produced a real gastronomic treat. Fortt's Bath buns were sent direct from Bath. They were not like the sawdust confections produced nowadays, but each bun was full of currants and small pieces of sugar, the under-side covered with a thick coating of sugar. The only other buns which rivalled these were the butter buns from Towyn in Merioneth, reproduced most successfully by Plant's of Bridgnorth from a recipe obtained by my grandfather. Maurice and I once made this journey to Swindon with the bearded postmaster of Chiseldon, Mr Last, in his pony and trap. It was a beautiful drive through the Hodson Woods and by Coate reservoir. It took us two hours to cover the four miles to Swindon.

Our routine during the last two Chiseldon holidays was greatly changed by the advent of a car. I returned from Aldro in late July 1931 to find a gleaming blue Morris Cowley tourer parked in the back garden at Hammersmith. It was a 1928 model, therefore second-hand. The petrol tank was situated immediately above the engine, which caused us some nervous moments in later days. Mother had bought the vehicle, presumably with a legacy from Grandmother who had died in 1929. She took a course of driving lessons at the British School of Motoring and was poised to drive us all to Chiseldon; there were no driving tests. Father insisted on travelling by rail, so he took the baggage train with him. We sped merrily out of London down the Kings Road to the Great West Road. We stopped at Theale, the other side of Reading, for lunch at a pub and I can still remember the tender roast lamb and young broad beans which they gave us. Then we set course for Chiseldon. In those days there was no return spring on the steering, so that if you turned round a corner, you had to straighten the wheel afterwards. Mother had often ridden a horse and forgot that the car would not straighten out by itself like a horse. We turned on to a side road on the Downs, where there was a high grass bank on the left. Forgetting to turn the steering wheel back, Mother mounted this bank and left us all perched at an angle of forty-five degrees. We found a farmer to pull us out with his tractor, but Mother lost her nerve and talked about selling the car. However, some friends who were staying with us persuaded her, after a week's rest, to take to the road again. She managed a slow drive to Marlborough and soon regained her confidence. She went on driving until she was well over eighty.

One holiday — it must have been 1932 — Goggy came to stay with us. I was, although only fourteen, keen to take the wheel. This I did with Goggy in the passenger seat. I soon learnt to drive and went out almost daily to practise on some lonely stretch of the road; these did exist in the Thirties. Emboldened by my success, I started to drive through Chiseldon village but was suddenly alarmed to see a policeman standing in the road. Foolishly I got out and changed places with Goggy. When we came up to the policeman he stopped us and asked my age. The result was a summons and my father had to pay a £2 fine. The policeman said that if we had not stopped, he would not have noticed. I suppose £2 was not too dear a price for learning how to drive.

# CHAPTER IV

## Shrewsbury

There was never any question about which school I should attend after Aldro. The family had been to Shrewsbury generation after generation, probably since the Bevans migrated there in about 1660. The school was originally the town grammar school, established by Edward VI in 1552 to replace the monastic establishment. My grandfather and great-grandfather were educated in the Tudor buildings opposite the railway station, now the town library. In 1882 the Revd H. W. Moss, Head-master, had moved the school across the river to a beautiful site overlooking the town. This comprised a workhouse, which became the main building, where teaching took place, and other buildings which were turned into boarding houses. The new school had been in oper-ation for fourteen years when my father went there in 1898. One of his contemporaries was Basil Oldham, who in 1911 founded and built his own House, Oldham's Hall, which overlooked the cricket field on one side and the river on the other.

When I arrived in 1932 Basil Oldham had had a breakdown and was forced to hand over his House to S. S. Sopwith, the senior English master. Whereas Oldham had been a highly emotional character, given to romantic relationships with his boys, Sopwith was the very opposite; urbane and civilised with an attractive sense of humour, he was exactly what the House needed.

My father took me down to Shrewsbury and New Boys' Tea in Oldham's Hall. As I automatically munched the cucumber sandwiches, not feeling at all hungry, I gaped at the enormous size of the monitors, who were sent in to introduce us to the House. The Head of House, John Malins, a great 'tweak' (as senior boys were called), seemed kindly disposed, as did James Hill and Donovan Allen, both to become clergy-men in later years. I always admired these monitors of my first year;

they were civilised and although it was the custom for monitors to give corporal punishment, they never abused their power. The House had recently emerged from a 'reign of terror' in which the Head of House, taking advantage of Basil Oldham's incapacity, laid about everyone and beatings were continuous. In my time there was no bullying. Instead of being herded together in dayrooms, we lived in studies which we shared with three to five other boys, each study comprising a cross-section of the House and ruled by a Study Monitor. We slept in bedrooms, not dormitories, under a Bedroom Monitor who was allowed to beat with a slipper. Malins once gave a boy the alternative of six with the slipper or forty with the toothbrush; he chose the latter but regretted it. After a week or two new boys (or 'scum') were give a 'colour exam'. This was a test on school general knowledge, such as the names of the statues over the library door, nicknames of masters, parts of the school site and many other details. The questions were very searching and the price of failure was a beating. I dreaded colour exams almost more than School Certificate or Cert A.

I had not only a brand new Housemaster but Headmaster as well. H. H. Hardy succeeded Canon H. A. P. ('Bob') Sawyer in September 1932. Bob had been a most lovable character but was extremely absent-minded. There are many stories about him, but I think the best concerns a visit by an old boy, who was asked: 'Let me see: was it you or your brother who was killed in the War?'. Hardy was a man of entirely different style: a former major in the Rifle Brigade, he had been Head-master of Cheltenham. He had a military bearing and a small moustache which invited the obvious comparison. At the beginning of the 'Tucks' run, in which the whole school and many of the staff partici-pated, Hardy appeared in running shorts, ready to take part. The whole assembly raised its arms in the Nazi salute. Hardy's rule was the exact opposite of Bob Sawyer's: he had everything meticulously organized; printed forms and circulars abounded. His staff never got on with him, but as boys we were less affected. I was sometimes invited to Kingsland House, the Headmaster's house, for tea or, later on, dinner, when I once met Dean Inge. Hardy's son, Tim, sang in my choir, The Quatford Singers, in the late Thirties; he is now the famous actor, Robert Hardy.

To return to my early days in Oldham's. Among my contemporaries were Michael Charlesworth, who, except for two interludes, spent his whole life in the service of the school, ending up as second master, Patrick Day, who became an academic and was a lecturer at Keele University and John Ferguson, later a distinguished surgeon.

Having won a scholarship, I was placed in the fifth form, 'Classical VB', destined to sit for School Certificate at the end of my first year. My form master was the Revd J.O. ('Joe') Whitfield, who was also a House-master. He was not an inspiring teacher, but he made us work. The School Certificate required five passes, but if you wished to matriculate, that is enter a university, you had to gain five credits. I took seven subjects and secured six credits. A contrast this to the modern GCSE candidates who often pass in ten or twelve subjects. We did, however, study our work in greater depth. I know a girl who recently gained a degree in classics, reading set books which I had read at Aldro.

To begin with I found difficulty in getting through the seemingly enormous quantity of work set each day. We had an hour and a half set aside for preparation, or 'Top Schools' as it was called, where all the junior boys worked in the House dining hall under a monitor. It was nearly always necessary to prolong this period of study into so-called free time; in fact most of my day which was not taken up by class, music or games, was spent working on my own. We had not been trained to do this at Aldro; hence my difficulties.

An additional problem was the school custom of fagging or 'douling' as it was called. All boys in their first two years were known as 'scum' or 'douls' (from the Greek doulos, a slave). If a monitor tapped the hot water pipes in Headroom (the monitors' sanctum) the sound could be heard all over the House and all douls had to rush to Headroom. The last to arrive was given the job. A large slice of one's time could be lost in this way. The custom has now happily been discontinued.

I was never forced to play more than a modicum of games; an occasional football game in my first two terms and house runs were the main requirements. Otherwise the sensible rule was that we had to take exercise by doing a 'change' every day. This could be an organised game, a run by oneself or a visit to the swimming baths. I joined the Boat Club, so that I never played cricket.

Social life at Shrewsbury was regulated by a strict code. You were not supposed to be friendly with a boy from another year, nor indeed from another House. Each year was strictly segregated and marked by variations in dress. The small boys wore Eton collars, two-year olds wore collars with rounded tips, three-year olds had pointed tips, four-year olds had longer points and 'tweaks', that is school colour men, university scholars, school monitors and praepostors, soft collars. On weekdays everyone wore a blue suit, but on Sundays it was Eton jackets for the new scum, top hats and tails for the rest. The praepostors and school monitors wore butterfly collars and carried walking sticks or umbrellas. Areas where you could walk were carefully delineated; only tweaks could walk on the grass or wear a handkerchief in the breast pocket.

We had our own school language which contained some picturesque words: 'lift' meant being above yourself, 'grip' meant steal, a bicycle was a 'bincey', 'sap' was work, 'to wazz' was to feel nervous, 'stiff' meant overloaded, particularly with work, 'ticket' was the school certificate, precursor of O level. A typical Salopian sentence would be: 'I'm stiff for sap. My form brusher (= master) has gripped all my notes and I am wazzing for the ticket.' All this, like the douling, has completely passed away.

One particular time waster, as it seemed to me, was the Corps, or Officers' Training Corps, to give it its full title. After our first year we were all expected to join it. Officially it was voluntary, but my Housemaster made it quite clear that if I aspired eventually to high office in the House, I had better join up. Not being of a rebellious, or even independent turn of mind, I complied. Hoping that it might provide an interesting diversion, I joined the band as a drummer. I duly learnt how to produce a roll, but the music which issued from a bugle and drum band did little to satisfy my artistic cravings. Fortunately in about my second year a brass band replaced the bugles and I was given the E flat horn to play. This instrument was not difficult and had an interesting counter-melody in Colonel Bogey. Soon, however, I was changed to the B flat baritone, an instrument of about the same size as a three-month-old baby, which had to be carried in a similar manner. I believe that it is now obsolete and perhaps, — who knows? — I am one of the few remaining exponents of this instrument still alive. The band gave me my first lessons in the playing of brass instruments which stood me in good stead when, many years later, I had to teach elementary brass at Downside and elsewhere. I even learnt how to play on the march without wobbling off the note.

I have referred to the Corps as a time waster. In theory we were training to be officers in the next war, but the training was woefully inadequate. The uniforms, with their wind-on puttees, were those of 1914–18, as were the drill, tactics and Lewis guns, which always jammed after firing ten rounds. When war actually came nothing I had to do seemed remotely connected with the Corps. The fact that I had passed Cert A carried no weight when I entered the Royal Artillery in 1942. The only benefit I received, apart from the band, was the knowledge that if I could eat the food provided at OTC camp, I could eat anything.

My first music teacher at Shrewsbury was W. H. Moore, who had previously taught my uncle Temple when he was there before the Great War. His nickname was Black Death, but his character did not correspond to his name; he was a gentle person, much liked by everyone.

Although in fact Director of Music, he was not known by that name and taught mathematics besides music. He was one of the last part-time music masters who had little music to direct. After my first year he retired and was replaced by Mr J. Barham Johnson; 'Johnnie' (his somewhat unimaginative nickname) had been at Bryanston, a much more 'arty' school than Shrewsbury; he had not prospered. At Shrewsbury, however, he did set about the organisation of a music department and the provision of music other than instrumental lessons. From him I learnt the chorus parts of Handel's Messiah, was encouraged to compose and even conduct the school orchestra. The Christmas concert became a serious affair and works by Stanford and Parry replaced the old music-hall numbers. I rapidly became allergic to Stanford, but we did attempt the works of greater composers. It was unfortunate that Johnnie was not a gifted teacher; he never made me work and much of my organ lesson would be taken up by his playing to me. Naturally inclined to inactivity, I drifted into a careless keyboard technique which I never really remedied in future years. He did, nevertheless, fire my enthusiasm for music and for this I am eternally grateful.

Shrewsbury had a distinguished reputation for classical scholarship. This dated from the early nineteenth century under the headmastership of Samuel Butler, followed by Benjamin Hall Kennedy and H. W. Moss. The honours boards in the main school building abounded with Craven and Ireland scholarships and other university honours. On the classical side, the largest in the school, we had as our teachers J. M. Street, R. W. Moore (later to be Headmaster of Harrow), Stacey Colman, previously a Fellow of Queen's, and H. N. Dawson. All these could be described as the cream of the classical teaching profession and Geoffrey Lane (who was in the sixth form with me and later became Lord Chief Justice) told me that he never learnt anything at Cambridge which he had not already learnt at Shrewsbury. I cannot claim this in my own case, but then I was not as clever as Lane and perhaps Oxford is a superior university. Harry Dawson, although a first class scholar, was unable to teach us much because he could not keep order. It became a tradition to 'mill' during a Dawson period and many were the outrageous tricks we played. The most notorious was the 'six o'clock express'. As soon as the bell sounded six, everyone would bang down his desk lid and shout 'Take your seats'; while some blew whistles, others simulated the escape of steam and puffs from the departing train. Poor Harry Dawson would beseech us to be quiet, but that only made things worse; on one occasion he actually burst into tears. Strangely enough, many years later I was told that there had been a complete change and that every word uttered by 'The Dawson' was received with rapt attention. I often wonder how he did it.

I have said that in the fifth form Joe Whitfield made me realise what work meant. The pressure in the next form, the Remove, was increased by our new form master, Roger Wilson. His penchant for setting up piles of work was well known throughout the school and added a new word to the school language; to be 'Rogered for Sap' meant to be extremely 'stiff' for it. Shortly after I moved out of his form, Roger became a clergyman and ended as Bishop of Chichester. My third year, in the Lower Sixth, under R. St J. Pitts-Tucker, later Headmaster of Pocklington School, was less arduous. He was an exponent of muscular Christianity and founded the school scout troop. In Upper Sixth B, in my fourth year, we had R. W. Moore, an ex-scholar of Christ Church and author of a book on Latin, Greek and Sanskrit syntax. He was very precise and expected us to be the same. It was from this form that Tony Chenevix-Trench won a scholarship to Christ Church at the age of seventeen. Tony was the most accomplished scholar of my own age that I ever knew. He told me that grammar was beaten into him at his prep school. Perhaps that is why in later years, when he was Headmaster of Bradfield, Eton and Fettes, he gained the reputation of being a fierce beater. However that may be, I always knew him as a mild, friendly boy, too small in stature to instil fear into anyone. He died while still at Fettes, possibly because of ill-treatment previously suffered as a Japanese prisoner of war.

The daily routine at Shrewsbury was busy and by modern standards spartan. On rising in the morning everyone had to take a cold shower or 'swill'; we stood on a board which released a jet of freezing water. Oldham's was the only House to sport such luxurious swills; others had to stand under a pipe which protruded from a wall. Next there was the walk (or run) to chapel; the smaller boys would enter below the belfry where an elderly but benign clergyman, known as 'The Tush' ticked off the names. Once a resourceful boy, finding his way barred because he was late, besought the old man: 'Sir, surely you're not going to shut me out of the House of the Lord?' 'Come in, boy, come in' was the reply. After a fifteen-minute service we went into first lesson, a forty-minute period of work before the walk back to the House for breakfast. Hardy moved the chapel service to a post-breakfast hour, but not until I had endured several terms of the old regime.

The food was better than at Aldro, but only slightly, so I was greatly surprised one day when Mr Sopwith's mother-in-law, a Mrs Brawn, died. The next day the whole House for the first and only time, was served brawn for breakfast. It was in Oldham's that I tasted baked beans on toast for the first time. Meals were taken in the separate houses and catering arranged by the Housemaster's wife, with her own staff of cooks and maids. Each House was run as a private concern by the Housemaster, who kept the profits after paying over a set sum to the school. The days of communal feeding did not dawn until the Sixties. Unlike Aldro, we were not condemned to starvation. If we felt hungry we could visit the school shop, where for a small sum we could on a half-holiday devour eggs, bacon, sausages and other delicacies. We were not allowed to go 'down town' without permission, which was seldom given. When we did go, we had to wear a straw hat with house hat band; only the sixth form could go without permission and they wore a black band. Visits to the Granada cinema were strictly forbidden. Tony Chenevix-Trench once decided to spend the afternoon there, but when the lights went up for the interval, there was the Headmaster sitting directly behind him. Sometimes tradesmen used to visit the school site with vans full of wares for sale. Among these was Mr Sidoli, the ice-cream maker. We had a long speech from Hardy, who loved a pompous turn of phrase, to the effect that we should 'refrain from patronising the vehicle driven by Mr Sĭdōlĭ or Sĭdŏlī, the itinerant vendor of ice-creams.'

Although we went to chapel compulsorily every weekday and twice on a Sunday, not to mention the voluntary 'early service', we were taught little about our religion. There were house prayers ('dicks') every night, including a hymn which I usually played, but my knowledge of Christianity had deepened little since my childhood days. On the classical side the weekly religious knowledge class usually took the form of preparing and translating a passage from the Greek New Testament, and was no different from an ordinary Greek class. In the Upper Sixth, our form master was a Unitarian and felt unable to teach us any theology. Probably few of the staff were practising Anglicans, although many attended the school services. Most of what I learnt was gleaned from sermons in chapel, and sometimes I had to glean very hard. The fact is that there was no systematic religious teaching in the school. We had a succession of school chaplains, a necessity arising from the fact that Hardy was the first lay Headmaster in the school's history. Most of these were ineffective: the first, 'Wee-Wee' Cross, I knew only by sight; the second, the Revd A. L. E. Hoskyns-Abrahall ('Ally-ha-ha') I liked personally, but he tried to get too close to the boys and many, including myself, were frightened off. There was no suggestion of immorality, but boys are apt to be scared of intimate emotional relationships with their schoolmasters. Hoskyns eventually became a Bishop.

As was inevitable in a single sex school, there was a degree of homosexuality between boys. This is not to say that there was much immorality; there was probably very little, but it was normal for a boy to be 'crashed' on a younger one. Sometimes 'tea notes' containing messages of love would be exchanged. I was in love with several boys, one of whom is now a bishop, but I do not suppose that they knew anything about it: I never wrote a 'tea-note'.

Perhaps the best thing Hardy did, at least in the boys' eyes, was to institute 'Country Expeditions'. We lived on the edge of the most beautiful countryside in the British Isles, the Welsh border. The Stretton Hills, Corndon, the Breiddens and Pontesford Hill were within easy cycling distance. Two days in the summer term were designated as whole holidays and we were encouraged to go out in groups riding the 'bincies' which those normally unprivileged were allowed to use on these occasions. I sported an ancient but solid Raleigh, which was known as the 'scooter with a stone seat.' Of course there was the danger that we would ride out to a remote pub and spend the day there. Twenty years later half the boys might have returned to school dead drunk, but on the whole we were a law-abiding community in the Thirties. During my last term I did visit a pub in the company of the Head of School and several other eminent personages but we were all tweaks and considered ourselves above the law in this matter.

My last two years at school were happy ones. In September 1936 I was given the post of Choregus, which meant head of the choir and of music generally. I became increasingly interested in the choir work, something which I must have inherited from my mother. I decided to form a small choir of my own, which performed mainly sacred music in neighbouring villages. We finished the year by performing Bach's Cantata *Wachet auf* in Quatford church with orchestra; this was my first experience of conducting and I began to look for further opportunities of this sort. The Quatford Festival, as it was called, took place annually until 1940. The standard of the choir was high, or so I thought, although the ages of the singers, thirteen to eighteen, were not the best for vocal quality. Of orchestral playing I knew very little, nor was I competent to choose visiting soloists. Some of these made the most extraordinary noises. We managed, nevertheless, to perform several works and I received no complaints. From time to time, when 'Johnnie' was ill, it was my job to play the organ for school services. One morning, not having anything special to play afterwards, I gave out the first line of a popular song *Pennies from Heaven*, which I then disguised with Bach-like counterpoint and fugal entries. All the boys recognised it, but the Headmaster was blissfully unaware of anything amiss.

The first term of my final year, 1936–7, ended with my journey to Oxford. My tutors were understandably worried by my musical interests, which they feared might take too much time from classical studies. My form master, Jimmy Street, took me aside and warned 'there are two things which ruin a classical scholar – music and drink'. My Latin was good but Greek on the whole poor. Although I could write good Latin verses, I knew that I would have to rely on my English essay to secure any award which might be on offer. How well I remember the examination, sitting in the hall of New College, staring at the electric lights which protruded from the walls like false teeth. I decided to write down everything I knew in the essay, as in the examination for the Chinese Civil Service. The title set was 'Scholarship', about which I had written the previous week for Sopwith. The *viva voce* was not very taxing, and I remember even making a joke — a dangerous thing for a schoolboy to do in front of dons, but they all laughed, so perhaps it was funny. A week later came a telegram to say that I had won an Open Exhibition at Queens, my father's old college. I was now a tweak and could wear a soft collar.

I suppose I worked for the next two terms, but the pressure was relaxed. 'Mossy' Moore organised a Greek play, Aeschylus' Agamemnon, for which I was commissioned to write the chorus music and lead the singing. I still have the score, which resembles Gregorian chant more than anything else. At about this time, I received the surprising news that I, together with Michael Charlesworth, had been made a praepostor *honoris causa* for services to the school music. This, as far as I knew, had never happened before, praepostors normally being not merely members of the Upper Sixth, but also Heads of Houses. I must confess that I took great pride in my butterfly collar and walking stick, ridiculous though they would be thought today. The other members of my bedroom laughed heartily at my efforts to push the studs through the starched holes of the new collar. I expect they were jealous.

My final week of school life was spent at Corps camp at Tidworth. Only one thing of note occurred: I was promoted acting lance-corporal on the last day. I had been unique in being the only praepostor to remain a private for the whole of my Corps career; I hurriedly sewed on the single stripe before catching the train for home.

# CHAPTER V

*Growing up at Home*

It is now time to return to 1932 and survey events at home. Towards the end of my time at Aldro, on returning from my scholarship examination at Shrewsbury, I developed a high temperature. It turned out to be scarlet fever, in those days a serious disease. Luckily I was at home and home comforts did much to palliate the rigours of my illness. Enormous efforts were made to isolate me; I was moved to the best bedroom, where the Bishop of London had sat to watch the Boat Race; a disinfected sheet was hung over the door and I was attended by a young and pretty nurse. I was too young to appreciate her fully and she seemed to be more interested in a young man called 'Ginger' who frequently appeared opposite our house on the Surrey side of the river. After about six weeks I was pronounced cured, but ordered to 'take things easily'. I needed no pressure to obey that order and allowed myself to be waited on by all and sundry. I returned to Aldro for my last term bearing the delightful news that I was not allowed to play games. A boy called Burton, who had also been ill, was sent with me for daily walks along the sea front at Eastbourne where we surveyed the bathing beauties who adorned the scenery: much better than cricket.

We spent the summer holidays at Chiseldon, for the last time. I had always loved the village, which nestled in a hollow and was full of thatched cottages. I used to wake up in the morning to see these wreathed in a thin mist, with smoke coming from the little chimneys and the school bell ringing. In our early days there we saw few cars; the traffic was horse-drawn except for one prosperous farmer who clattered by in a solid-tyred Morgan. Opposite the vicarage was a blacksmith, whose hammer and anvil I can still hear in my memory. In his garden the well was still in daily use and Maurice and I would go over and draw up the water. In the house we had no electric light. Paraffin gas was installed at the end of our time, but for most of our visits we had to make do with candles. As at Quatford, these were put on a table for the grown-ups to light themselves to bed. I would often lie in bed and hear them come upstairs, the flickering lights casting ghostly shadows on the walls; indeed ghosts seemed to lurk in every corner, but I never saw one.

After my first term at Shrewsbury I returned to Hammersmith for the family Christmas. One of its features was a concert which Maurice and I gave for several years running in our house before an invited audience. We used to sing solos and duets, act sketches and recite, to the delight of a somewhat uncritical audience. Another annual event was the Bishop of London's children's party; this took place on 28th December, Holy Innocent's day, thus endowing us guests with an attribute wholly undeserved. Dressed in their best finery the children of the diocesan clergy gathered at Fulham Palace and queued up to meet their host. Bishop Winnington-Ingram was not like one of our modern bishops, who dress as much like curates as they can; he crammed on everything he had. Dressed from head to foot in a purple tail suit with gaiters, his top half was decorated like a Christmas tree with stars, medals and orders. He would greet us reclining on a sofa and every time he spotted a pretty girl (or boy) he would pull her down to him and smother her with kisses. He once did this to my mother on the stairs at St Dunstan's Vicarage, but that is another story. I need hardly say that his Lordship was a bachelor. After this welcoming ceremony dancing began. We were all expected to find partners and woe betide those who failed; you could not be a 'wallflower' for long without being set on by some haggard archdeacon's wife and swept into the fray. The party ended with the post-horn galop, in which the Bishop took part; 'Sir Roger de Coverley' and 'For he's a jolly good fellow' followed; this earned the annual response from our host: 'You're all jolly good fellows'. The band, which consisted, it seemed, of Chelsea pensioners playing obsolete saxophones, then played the concluding voluntary and the guests dispersed.

The year 1933 brought two important events: one was the birth of my youngest brother, Christopher, fifteen years younger than I, and the other was my first meeting (except for a childhood encounter) with my future wife. In April my father took me for a walking holiday on the Gower coast in South Wales. We stayed at the Caswell Bay Hotel and had the whole place to ourselves, except for one other guest; this was the famous Bishop Bevan of Swansea and Brecon. He was related to us in a vague sort of way, but I was never able to discover how. He was connected with the Bevans of Hay Castle, who appear in Kilvert's

Diary. The Bishop spent long hours discussing the ecclesiastical problems of his diocese, so I was not able to contribute much; but I remember his stentorian voice, which filled the hotel; there is now a statue of him in Brecon Cathedral.

In the summer Christopher was born. At first neither Maurice nor I were greatly affected by this, but when I returned home from school, I experienced my first close contact with a baby. I was often left to look after him and gradually grew very fond of him. I used to change his napkins and give him his bottle, a useful rehearsal for looking after my own children. Mother felt that at forty she was too old to look after babies; in consequence Christopher was usually farmed out to surrogate mothers and saw little of his parents. He was sent away to a nursery school as a boarder at the age of, I think, six. This of course was much too young and helped to estrange him from his home. I saw little of him, being away from home a great deal myself, and so we gradually lost contact. Now he lives in Scotland and we conduct a desultory correspondence.

Chiseldon being no longer available, we spent the summer holidays at Quatford; not at the Castle, however, because my grandfather was there and did not relish an invasion by so many visitors. My parents rented a house in the village, the Chantry, from Father's younger sister, Gwen Baldock. She and her three children, Rupert, Mollie and Dick, moved into the stables, which were reasonably habitable during August and September, but impossible in the winter. In 1933 Rupert was ten, Mollie nine and Dick eight; their father had died soon after Dick's birth and my aunt was left to bring up her family with no money except what Grandfather allowed her. The Chantry was one of his houses and she lived there rent free. At first a gulf separated us: the Baldocks were much younger and were Roman Catholics, a religion about which I knew very little and was deeply suspicious. My father told me that Catholics worshipped the Virgin Mary and that the priests he had seen in Brittany never washed their necks. I had fixed up an extension speaker from our wireless set in their house, but they never used it. I think my cousins regarded us as a dangerous Protestant influence and the loud speaker as the voice of the devil. For many weeks, therefore, we remained aloof. Feeling that I should make an effort to be sociable, I hailed Mollie in the drive one day: 'Would you like to come for a walk?' She seemed attracted by the idea; we did not walk very far, no further than Drewetts sweet shop round the corner. 'Why don't you go to Evans instead of Drewetts?' asked Mollie. 'Because Mr Drewett is a churchman' I replied. This pompous remark, which I had often heard from the lips of my parents, was never forgotten. Mollie reminded me of it fifty years later. At the end of the holidays I accompanied Mollie to her first boarding school, the Dominican convent at Brewood. She was never happy there; altogether she went to five different schools and hated all of them; in fact, although we ran a school together in later years and she was married all her life to a schoolmaster, she always protested that she loathed schools.

For one event during these holidays I became the hero of the hour. We were bathing in Dudmaston Pool, a lake in the neighbourhood, with Pippin's aunt, Ruth Baker. She was not a strong swimmer and while we were dressing on the bank, she began to get into difficulties, crying out and splashing. Being the only member of the party still in a bathing dress, I jumped in, circled round her and gave her a push. This moved her to a place where she could touch the bottom and she climbed up the bank. It was a small thing; I knew nothing about life saving and would have been useless in a real emergency. Ruth, however, was profusely grateful and gave me an inscribed silver cigarette case.

It is not necessary to go into great detail about the remaining years before the war. In 1934 my father took another locum, this time in Devonshire, whence I made my first journey abroad. With a school party, conducted by the school chaplain, Hoskyns-Abrahall, I travelled to Oberammergau for the Passion Play. We spent a day in Munich which was decked out with flags for a visit by Hitler. Huge banners, emblazoned with swastikas, hung from all the buildings; we drank our 'hell' and 'dunkel' in beer gardens; I played the overture to an oratorio 'The Transfiguration', which I had written at school, on the organ at the Deutsches Museum and I began to smoke cigars: everyone was smoking, even the policemen directing the traffic. The next time I visited Munich was sixty years later and I thought the place had sadly declined. Everyone had become politically correct; there were no cigars and the sausages I ate for lunch tasted of nothing at all. The Passion Play was magnificent – at least everyone said so – and certainly the crowd scenes, in which the whole village participated, were impressive. I was, however, only sixteen, a Protestant and seated a long way towards the back of the audience; the seat was hard and my bottom was aching. I inspected the extravagantly Rococo village church, which gave my puritanical prejudices a shock. I felt more at home in our anglican service held in a hut, where all the chairs were inscribed 'Löwenbräu'. Sailing down the Rhine from Mainz to Koblenz was much more to my taste; the towns were, like Munich, festooned with flags, for Hitler had visited the previous day.

Grandfather died in the summer of 1935 and Maurice and I attended his funeral at Quatford dressed in our Shrewsbury tails and top hats. At the funeral tea afterwards my mother was furious because Auntie Cecil played host and poured out the tea.

After term we spent our last summer holiday away from Quatford. This time the locum was a village near Olney called Emberton and we spent an idle time boating and fishing on the River Ouse. I should have gone to Corps Camp, but managed to display, on the eve of our departure, signs of an oncoming stomach upset. The Matron, fearing, I imagine, that she might have to spend the next few days clearing up after me, instead of enjoying her holiday, took the quick way out and dosed me with castor oil. The result was dramatic; by the next morning I felt like a drawn turkey, but it was worth it to miss camp. While at Emberton I passed my driving test, in the year that they were instituted; I drove our old 1928 Morris and double de-clutched to the examiner's satisfaction. I even had to know the signs given with the whip of a horse-drawn vehicle. After this my mother took a rest from driving and I was at the wheel every day.

We all smoked cigarettes and on the day before our departure from Emberton we had to dig up all the cigarette ends from the lawn. I will not say that we filled twelve basketfuls, but there were a great many of them. Except for Maurice and me, all those who dug up the cigarette ends are now dead, but none of them of lung cancer.

Apart from the constitutional upheavals, 1936 was an uneventful year for me. My main memories are of royal occasions, for two of which I had to parade with the band; first to hear Edward VIII proclaimed King in January. His names went through my head to the first two lines of the tune of the carol 'Unto us is born a son' which they fitted exactly: 'Edward Albert Christian George, Andrew Patrick David.' Previously we had all been suddenly released from school for the funeral of King George V and my parents were slightly disconcerted to find two sons on the doorstep, needing food and a trip next day up to central London. We managed to find standing room in Hyde Park, but so far back that we could see nothing but the plumes on the helmets of those passing in the procession. The following November saw the abdication and a second trip into town, following my B flat baritone, to proclaim George VI. All the talk was of approaching war; Hitler had occupied the Rhineland but no one was ready to face him. Disarmament had been government policy during the early Thirties, but now was reversed. Although we had to betray many of our European friends in the process, it would plainly have been disastrous to have attempted to resist Hitler with inadequate resources. The Opposition and left-wing thinkers, of whom there were many, were all bleating for a show of force. They were particularly vicious in 1938 at the time of the Munich

Agreement but the fact remains that we were badly defeated in 1940, when we had been re-arming for several years; what would have happened if we had gone to war in 1936 or 1938? It was then that I began to realise that I might have to follow my parents' generation to service in the trenches. All my contemporaries were similarly affected and an air of unreality began to cloud our lives and preparation for our careers.

Meanwhile Aunt May had died and left my mother a considerable sum, which she proceeded to spend with enthusiasm. The garden at Quatford sprouted exotic flowers, the Morris Cowley was replaced by a Standard 14 and for a short time we had a butler at the castle. Mother generously bought me a wooden hut which was erected in the garden. It overlooked the village and was a considerable eyesore to the beholder, rearing its ugly roof above the mellow sandstone walls. But it gave me a wonderful sense of independence. I could spend all my time in it, even sleep there if I chose, or I could entertain friends without disturbing others; these were all male — I was still shy of girls.

My mother had plans for me for a free year, either between Shrewsbury and Oxford, or at the end of my university studies; she used to hint darkly about my going abroad 'to sow my wild oats'. It was plain that she did not know the meaning of this phrase. I am sure that if I had populated the Shropshire countryside with offspring, as Uncle Goggy was reputed to have done in Malaya, she would not have approved. I was to go abroad, to Uncle Hughe, now Ambassador in Turkey, and, I suppose, find some young ladies in Ankara, with whom I could pursue her ambitions. Of course Mother meant merely that I should go out and see the world. But since I had won an exhibition, I had to go straight to Oxford, and when I had finished there, the war had begun. His Majesty gave me the chance of seeing the world later on, although in less agreeable circumstances; but I never managed to sow my wild oats.

Possibly connected with her wild oats idea was my mother's insistence that I should go out into society. During the autumn of 1938 I began to receive invitations from London hostesses to attend balls and other events at which their nubile daughters were presented for inspection by young males. At the end of my first year at university I was in no position to satisfy the hostesses' ambitions. Some of the girls were very attractive. I went to the Wheatland Hunt ball, escorting Diana Giffard. She did not really need my services, since she knew everyone and I, knowing no one and hating it all, spent most of the party propping up the wall. Diana eventually married Airey Neave, the Northern Ireland Secretary, who was tragically blown up by the IRA.

My father insisted that before going to university I should become a pipe-smoker. I suppose he thought that a pipe lent an air of dependability and *gravitas* to a young man, so I was packed off with a new pipe and a pouch of tobacco in the back seat of a friend's open tourer car. I suppose that if I was sick it would have gone over the side and not been any trouble. We sped up the Brown Clee hill, while I puffed madly. The wind blew all the ash and covered me with cinders, but I fought on. One pipe was enough, but I persevered on successive days until in a few weeks I was a confirmed disciple of Mr Baldwin, whose 'thoughts grew in the aroma of this particular tobacco'. I suppose all this had one good effect: I never smoked cigarettes.

# CHAPTER VI

$\clubsuit$

# *Oxford*

Goggy drove me to Queen's for my first term at Oxford. My room was at the top of the Front Quad on the third floor. It was small and had a separate bedroom next door. There were several other undergraduates on the same floor but I never remember seeing them; they were all north countrymen, a speciality of the College, and never came out of their rooms; they worked all day and half the night. I had a gas fire with a sofa and an armchair; behind the sofa was a table, but apart from bookshelves, there was no other furniture. It suited me and the rent was low. In those days we were waited on hand and foot: each staircase had a 'scout' who kept the rooms clean, called us in the morning, brought up breakfast, filled the boxes outside with coal and listened to our troubles; my first scout was called Jimmy Holmes. We could have a luncheon party with our tutor's permission; we could order whatever we liked from the kitchens and Jimmy would lay the table, bring up the food and serve it. I entertained my parents twice in this way, but it was expensive. Nevertheless my first term's 'batells', or college bill, amounted to no more than £35! Normally we had bread and cheese in Hall for lunch, but dinner was a formal affair which we were required to attend, wearing gowns, most evenings in the week. Morning Chapel was also nominally compulsory, but you could get out of it by reporting to the porter's lodge at Chapel time and then returning to your room for a leisurely breakfast.

In many ways we lived more comfortably than the present generation, but not in all: there were no lavatories nor washing facilities on the staircases. If we wanted a bath or needed to visit the lavatory, we had to walk across the quad in our pyjamas and descend to an underground cellar beneath the chapel.

Classical Honour Moderations was to be my first hurdle. This was a particularly arduous examination in Greek and Latin literature, taken during our fifth term. The syllabus was enormously wide, including Latin and Greek prose, verse and unseen translation, the complete works of Homer and Virgil, various Latin orations of Cicero, historical works of Livy and Tacitus, Greek dramas by Aeschylus, Sophocles, Euripides and Aristophanes, as well as a special subject which at my tutor's suggestion was Roman poetry. There were about fourteen papers in the examination. This was enough for a degree at most places, but not at Oxford. My tutor was a Scotsman, T. E. Wright, who was a martinet about work. Lectures were not compulsory and we soon learnt which were worth attending. I always went to Cyril Bailey's lectures. We had weekly 'collections', written tests on our week's work, with essays to write and read aloud at a weekly 'tutorial'. We were all expected to get 'firsts' in Mods and most of us did; I, however, did not. There were no upper seconds or lower seconds in those days; you gained a plain second.

I joined the college choir, which sang choral evensong twice a week, and I even played the organ occasionally. The real organist was Bernard Naylor, a fine musician and orchestral conductor, who eventually took over the Winnipeg Symphony Orchestra, but he was not interested in church music and found the college choir a bore. He spent most evenings in his room drinking and dispensing whisky. Once Maurice and I went to stay with him at his cottage at Hitcham, in Suffolk. We were called at 7.30 am with gin and tonic; the dose was repeated at breakfast, 11 am, 1 pm, 5 pm and 7 pm. After dinner we changed to whisky.

In spite of the freedom and attractions offered by Oxford, I was at first desperately homesick for Shrewsbury. I think this was also the case with my friends who were all scattered about various colleges. At first we used to meet once a week at a restaurant: Tony Trench, Robin Lorimer, Patrick Brock and others. Gradually, however, as we made new friends, we drifted further apart, meeting only occasionally for dinner in each other's colleges. I once invited Tony to dinner in Queen's only to find us faced with a special fasting meal for the unemployed; the menu was soup and dry bread.

Like London, Oxford in the Thirties was crowded with slow-moving, noisy, evil-smelling traffic. There were no pedestrian precincts. The worst horror was the ubiquitous bus:

> See its roar and hideous hum
> Indicat motorem bum

It was one of these which, just outside the college, ran down and

*RHB aged 2*

*Maurice and RHB*

*Mother (circa 1927)*

*Father (circa 1940)*

*St. Dunstan's Vicarage.*
*Back row: Father, Mother. Seated: Miss Bates, Granny, Grandfather (Bevan), Maurice, Bonzo*

*Uncle Hughe, Grandmother (Knatchbull-Hugessen), Mother (1925)*

*Quatford Castle*

*Aldro. Drill display*

*Choking back the tears.*
*Maurice's first term at Aldro*

*New scum at Shrewsbury (1932)*

*RHB and Maurice (1933)*

*Corps camp at Strensall (1934)*

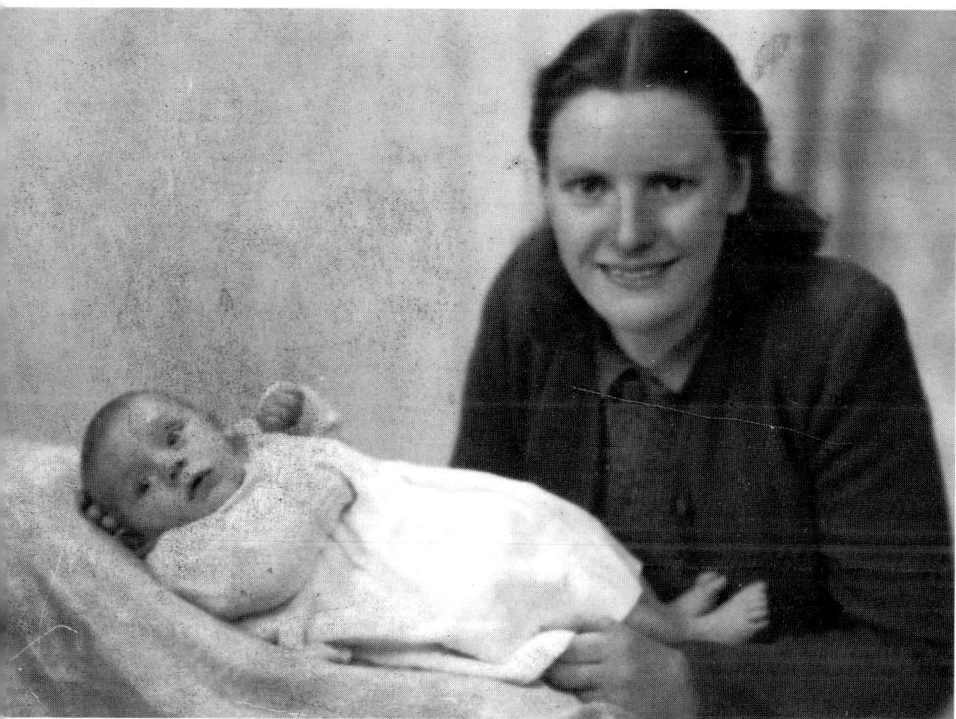

*Mollie with John (1947)*

*St. Mary's Newtown circa 1950. Fr. Roscoe Beddoes centre, RHB on his right*

killed Jack Edwards, the senior scholar of my year and winner of the 'Ireland'. Everyone was in a state of shock for several days; I played the organ for his memorial service.

All the winter both at Oxford and at home, I was reading for this ghastly Mods examination. When it was all over I decided to stop working for a while and planned the summer term of 1939 as a period of enjoyment and self-indulgence. It was the last term of peace.

During the previous winter I had met a girl, Dora Troup, who sang in the Eglesfield Choral Society. I had noticed her flashing her eyes in my direction while I was taking a rehearsal at Queen's and promptly invited her to tea. Dora was at St Hilda's, reading modern languages. My interest in her soon flared into a consuming passion; I had never known a girl before and the ways of women were strange to me. I was very wet behind the ears and must have been a source of amusement when she discussed me with her friends. Nowadays such romances usually end up in bed, but attractive as the idea might have seemed to me, I had no plans in that direction. I spent a deliriously happy Trinity term largely in her company. For my twenty-first birthday my mother had given me a Standard 9 car; this I took to Oxford, fitted with the regulation green light and garaged in Merton Street. I drove with Dora for hundreds of miles, ending with a joint outing with my mother and hers. It must have seemed as if we were planning to get married, but that was a castle in the air. Dora was ready to be married at any time, though not to me, as I had many years to go before I could support a wife. One day in the autumn we planned to meet in the West End. I emerged from the underground station to find Dora waiting with an RAF pilot, whom she introduced to me as her fiancé. I was mortified, but not for long. With the resilience of youth I soon recovered and even played the organ at her wedding. Dora would certainly not have fitted into the life of an Anglican clergyman: she was keen on horses and all her friends had similar interests. She once made me ride while staying at her house in Hampshire. The horse walked under a low tree and left me hanging on a branch like Absalom.

My twenty-first birthday party was held at Quatford Castle. My parents had the idea of throwing a great celebration to which the tenants and most of the village were invited. They all trooped up to the house where there were competitions, a fortune-teller and tea in a tent. I had to make a speech, as did the Vicar, Mr Morgan, and I was presented with a fitted suitcase and electric clock by the village. The car from my mother had been given to me a year in advance, so I was able to enjoy it for two years before wartime restrictions took it off the road. All these celebrations were, I suppose, intended to present me to the tenants as their future landlord. I always felt uncomfortable about this: was it right for a working parson to run an estate as a sideline? I wondered how my father felt dunning people for unpaid rents or hiring and firing employees and then often being absent when they might need him. Fortunately I never had to take on this responsibility. Quatford was not a profitable business; the outgoings always exceeded the income and my father was not a man of business. When it was eventually sold, the entire proceeds were needed to redeem the mortgage.

Such gloomy thoughts, however, did not disturb my tranquility as the weeks sped by and brought Armageddon ever nearer. Soon after my twenty-first birthday, I went with my mother, driving my little car, on a tour of South Wales: we spent most of our time in Pembrokeshire, ending up at St David's. It is amazing how the tourist trade has changed things. In those days, apart from in one or two expensive hotels on the coast, you could not get an evening meal in Wales after 6 pm.

The Quatford Festival was held as in the previous two years. As I collected the Headmaster of Shrewsbury, who wished to attend, his first words were 'It looks uncommonly like 1914'. He was right.

# CHAPTER VII

❧

# *War*

We were at Quatford when war was declared on 3rd September 1939. It was a Sunday and we were all at Matins in Quatford Church. The Vicar, Mr Morgan, stayed at home so that he could hear the announcement on the wireless and bring the news to the congregation. During the prayers, which I was leading, he came in and announced simply: 'War has been declared.'

We went home to the usual Sunday lunch, and indeed for many months everything continued as usual except for the pill-boxes and sandbags which appeared at every corner. Evacuees arrived from Liverpool and it was sad to see the poverty in which they lived. Many of the children were ignorant of the most elementary rules of sanitation. Mother fitted up a house for them in one of the outhouses but they were not happy. After a few months, when the German bombs never fell and our own aeroplanes were busy bombarding the enemy with leaflets, most of them went home. Later on we took in the families of airmen from the RAF station at Bridgnorth, but by that time I was away from home.

Mother had as her companion Auntie Cecil, who gave up her little house in Chelsea and moved to Quatford. Every evening they would play bézique together, but at 9 pm, just before the news, they would stand up to say the silent prayers recommended by the Archbishop of Canterbury and remain standing during the playing of the national anthems of the allies – a somewhat lengthy procedure. My father returned to London, where he shared the vicarage with Mr Ireson, the verger. I thought it strange that Mother should apparently feel quite happy about this arrangement, but she considered it her duty to look after Quatford and our permanent visitors rather than face the bombs with her husband.

With October came my return to Oxford. I was surprised to see on the platform at Banbury so many of my old friends. They were all waiting to be called up and had decided to follow their Oxford courses for as long as they could. I found that as a church student I was in a 'reserved occupation' and could stay and take my degree before entering a theological college. In order to hasten my training, I decided to read theology instead of 'Greats', thus cutting off a year of study before ordination.

During that summer vacation my college had completely changed. The dining hall and all the front quad had been taken over by a government ministry: the hall was full of small tables and the clatter of knives and forks was replaced by typewriters. Undergraduates, of whom there were not more than fifty, ate in the Junior Common Room ('Tabs' Room') and their own rooms, unless they were relegated to digs in the city, were in the Back Quad. I was lucky to be given one of these rooms, which I shared with Basil Moss. My tutor was E. C. Ratcliff, later to become Regius Professor of Divinity at Cambridge. He dressed on weekdays as a layman, wearing a gaudy tie over a blue shirt. The dog collar was reserved for Sundays. We were all surprised that his shirt was not brown, for he was a convinced fascist, an admirer of Mussolini, and had narrowly escaped internment under Regulation 18B. He was a learned liturgiologist and had helped to devise the coronation service in 1937. We had, living in Oxford, the Patriarch of the Assyrians, Mar Shimun. He would frequently go down to St Mary Magdalene church in the Cornmarket to say his Mass. Ratcliff was the only man in Oxford who knew the responses, which were in Aramaic, so he always served. After the rigours of Honour Mods I found theology relaxing and was able to follow some of my musical interests; these included organ lessons from William McKie at Magdalen. He taught me how to play tidily, an art which through inertia I have since lost. In theology all that seemed to be required of us was a weekly essay which we read to Ratcliff in his rooms. A good essay was rewarded by a glass of Marsala. Of course we were also supposed to read, attend certain lectures and visit the libraries. I found the course unrewarding. At the end of it I had a good knowledge of the Bible, or what was left of it after studying the German critics, a smattering of church history, ending at 461 AD, but little else. We never read the Fathers and knew little of the later developments of church doctrine. This was really my fault. We were supposed to read further into the subject on our own. Some others, such as Alan Webster, later Dean of St Paul's, managed to study privately Karl Marx as well as St Athanasius, but I preferred to practise the organ. In fact during this time I began to have doubts whether I wanted a clerical career; music seemed so much more to my taste. Such thoughts, however, I put behind me; at theological college, I hoped, closer contact with other ordinands might settle me.

The college chaplain, Victor Johnson, was an attractive personality, who devoted all his time to the undergraduates. He understood their problems, laughed at their stupidities but was always ready with advice; this was emphasised by a high falsetto laugh which could be heard throughout the college. He advised me to go to Westcott House, Cambridge, after taking my degree and there study under the great B. K. Cunningham. I had, however, another year to go at Oxford.

The war gradually moved nearer. Shortly before Dunkirk my old group of Shrewsbury singers, fortified by some boys from the Queen's College choir, gave a concert in the University Church. During those long, beautiful summer days of 1940 I used to look out of the window on to the peaceful churchyard of St Peter-in-the-East, feeling guilty that I was not with so many of my friends – on the beaches of Dunkirk. There were no air raids on Oxford and the only unusual sight was a queue stretching the whole length of the High of people trying to buy sweets at exorbitant prices from a company of sharks who had set up a black market in one of the shops.

During the Long Vacation I did some 'war work'; part of this consisted in helping in the garden at Quatford, where both the gardeners had left for the forces. With consequences which she could hardly have foreseen, Mother arranged for my cousin, Mollie Baldock, to work with me. We cut up wood, picked fruit and lifted potatoes. Mollie was only sixteen but we had much in common and became very friendly. Our activities were interrupted by a fortnight's forestry camp on the Clee Hills, organised by Shrewsbury School. Mollie returned home to Bridgnorth. From our position on the hill we could see the anti-aircraft fire and bombs dropping on Birmingham; but what we did not expect was a lone German plane off-loading its surplus bombs on Bridgnorth. While the casualties were light, much damage was done to houses and Mollie's mother, Aunt Gwennie, had all her windows blown out.

As September progressed, fears of invasion grew acute. We waited for the church bells to ring, a sign that the Germans had landed. One evening we suddenly heard the three bells of Quatford church. There was a hurried knock at the drawing room door and McClelland, our only remaining domestic, burst in with the news that the Germans had landed at Bewdley. My father turned to me: 'Go down and lock all the doors, Roger' he ordered. As I slid the bolts in the front door I wondered what was the purpose of the operation. Surely a Panzer division would have no difficulty against such an obstacle! Fortunately it was a false alarm. 'Perhaps the Germans forgot to change at Hartlebury' was Father's comment.

Not long afterwards my Aunt Dorothy, previously Miss Bates, our governess, arrived after being machine-gunned in a London street. She was closely followed by the wife of Tony Cato, one of Father's curates but now an army chaplain. Her sister soon joined the company and the castle was becoming fuller than ever. My mother was pleased; she did not like Aunt Dorothy, but the others were her great friends. They took all the burden of the housework off her shoulders and left her free to supervise the garden and help in the WRVS canteen in Bridgnorth. As for Maurice and me, we felt like strangers in our own home, but it was not to be for long.

At Christmas 1940, for the second year running, I was summoned to Oxford to conduct the Boar's Head ceremony. This dated from the thirteenth century, when a scholar of the college killed a wild boar by pushing a volume of Aristotle down its throat. Since then each Christmas Day the Boar's head had been borne into Hall in front of the assembled Fellows and guests. The choir processed up the centre of the Hall, singing the Boar's Head carol:

> Caput apri defero
> Reddens laudes Domino

The Provost then presented an orange, detached from one of the boar's tusks, to the head chorister, while the other singers each received a sprig of holly. The boys retired for lemonade and biscuits while the others settled down to the Boar's Head Feast. This was a normal dinner with turkey and plum pudding, but it was preceded by boar's head, slices of fatty ham, not unlike Bath Chap, eaten with mayonnaise sauce. I was too young to appreciate the wine, but no doubt it was good. All this was before the food shortage became acute. During the following year we celebrated the six-hundredth anniversary of the college's foundation. There was no wine then, but the ordinary hall dinner was supplemented by a dish of – sardines on toast!

At the beginning of the academic year 1940–41 I was appointed acting organist and choirmaster of the college. I was responsible for all the chapel music (evensong on Sundays and two weekdays) and had to direct rehearsals of the Eglesfield Music Society when Dr Reginald Jacques, as often happened, was unable to attend.

I enjoyed my last year at Oxford more than any other so far in my life. I realised later that training choirs was all I really wanted to do, but at the time I did not analyse my feelings very carefully. I think the choir improved while I was there; in fact Lord Elton, the pro-Provost, was heard to remark 'How is it that the choir has become so good?'. I composed an anthem for the sexcentenary of the College to words by Ratcliff and music much in the style of Stanford; I even wrote a chant book which was used for a few years.

During the same year I met Fergus O'Connor, the enterprising choir-master of St Mary and St John, Cowley. This was an extreme Anglo-Catholic church where they 'had everything': bells, incense, confession, crowning of the May queen and a staff of curates who wore lace cottas and cassocks with buttons down the front; they believed in Papal Infallibility and slid along the deep carpets of the vicarage, a purely bachelor establishment, as if they were on wheels. I always loved the Anglo-Catholics, but became deeply suspicious of their sincerity. I asked one of the curates why he did not become a Roman Catholic; he answered that he intended to, but was waiting to bring over as many as possible with him. A likely story.

Fergus O'Connor worked with me to produce my last musical en-terprise at Oxford. Our two choirs joined and we performed, among other things, Byrd's Great Service. Afterwards Professor Gunn, the professor of Egyptology, always ready for a joke, presented me with a cheque for £20, signed 'William Byrd'. When I had to leave the choir, I wept in the chaplain's room.

During the first two weeks of the Long Vacation I took the choristers, helped by Oxford friends, to a forestry camp near Quatford. It was hard because no one but I could cook. It was during this time that I heard that I had gained a second in theology and was now a BA. My father lost no time in recruiting me to help the depleted staff in the local churches and every Sunday I was preaching in surrounding villages. I gravely of-fended the parishioners of Astley Abbots by referring to an advertise-ment which was everywhere displayed in response to the German air raids on Britain. It stated simply 'HIT BACK'. No doubt it was rash of me, little more than a boy with no experience of the horrors of the war, to point out that hitting back was not what was advised in the gospels. There were complaints and I was not asked to preach there again.

I have said that in the early days of the war things at home continued much as in peacetime. We no longer brought servants with us from London but at the castle we were still waited on by two retainers, McClelland, who looked after the house and Mrs Leary (pronounced 'Larry' by us, but by no one else) who cooked. She was a very good 'plain' cook, as the description ran in those days: she could roast meat, make a stew or, to use her own phrase 'knock up a Queen's pudding'; she also made excellent cakes. As she was growing old, however, McClelland suggested that her sister, Mrs Hill, should come and take

Mrs Leary's place in alternate months. Mrs Hill was an expert: out of simple ingredients she could make every meal a banquet. I remember her delicious fish cakes, made with a white sauce instead of potato, rissoles with scrambled egg, rabbit mousse and countless other delicacies. War or no war, we lived like fighting cocks, eating food to rival the best hotel. It was not to last. When my mother's two friends, Doris Cato and Beryl Hutton arrived, the old retainers understandably decided to retire and let the younger ones take over. By the beginning of 1941 the old regime at Quatford, which had lasted since 1830, collapsed. We never again had servants. The whole family moved down to the kitchen and servants' hall. The upstairs living rooms were used by the RAF families, shortly to arrive. Everyone took on house or kitchen work except my father who throughout his life never even learnt how to boil an egg.

Rationing became severe; we were, for instance, allowed only a small lump of butter, less than quarter of a pound, to last the whole week. Mother used to put each person's ration on a plate with a flag bearing his name stuck into each lump. Mother hated rationing. She maintained that it was better to go without, rather than eat bread and scrape. So she ate all her butter ration on the first day. She kept geese in the field, so that we were never short at Christmas.

The time had now come for me to enter on the last stage of my education. In August 1941 I entered Westcott House, Cambridge. Those who had degrees in theology were not required to stay for the whole course. After only one year the dog collar would be awaiting me.

# CHAPTER VIII

### ❧

# *Cambridge and Conversion*

Westcott House in 1941 represented a cross section of the Church of England. Every possible shade of religious opinion was represented, from those who walked round the quadrangle saying their rosary to those who did not believe in baptismal regeneration. It was all held together by the magnetic personality of a great man, Canon B. K. Cunningham. 'B.K.' or 'Professor', as we students called him, was an old man when I knew him. He was immensely experienced in dealing with young men and seemed to know what was in their minds before they said anything. This was just as well, since B.K. was almost stone deaf and could only hear with the aid of a primitive machine, a box which was connected by various wires to his ears. When you sat next to him in the refectory, he would put this box by your place and order you to say something; on one occasion I told him a funny story – at least I thought it was – but there was no reaction; while he twisted the knobs I had to repeat the story in a loud voice three or four times; everyone else fell silent until I had to confess that it was no longer funny.

In the chapel we had Matins, Holy Communion and Evensong every day except Sundays. We used a different rite each day: Monday was the Church of Scotland prayer book, Tuesday the Book of Common Prayer, Wednesday 1549 (why? I wondered) and so on through the week. On Sundays there were no services as we were encouraged to attend the church of our choice in the town. Most of the students went to a low church, where all the clergy wore moustaches; I went to Mass at Fisher House, where Fr. Alfred Gilbey presided over his flock of old Gregorians and Amplefordians. They surrounded his breakfast table after Mass, drinking sherry. I thought them a queer lot.

Besides attending services we were required to conduct them. This happened at the Leper Chapel, a small Norman church on the

Newmarket road. We also officiated at various village churches around Cambridge and at Addenbrooke's Hospital. It was there on one occasion that I was attempting to inspire the men's surgical ward with a scholarly commentary on St Paul's first epistle to the Corinthians, when I looked up from my manuscript to find every patient with the *News of the World* propped up before him. When I went round to give spiritual comfort, I received only monosyllabic replies to my questions, until I reached one patient from whom I could elicit nothing; he turned out to be dead.

All through this time I was able to keep my organ practice going: I was preparing a recital which I gave later at Queen's, Oxford, and was allowed to use the organ both at St Catherine's and King's Colleges. Harold Darke, who was keeping the seat warm for the regular organist, Boris Ord, kindly allowed me to play at King's and many are the sightseers who must have had their eardrums beaten in by the 32 ft bombard.

All this time I was increasingly agitated by thoughts of Roman Catholicism. During the previous year Mollie and I had become deeply attached to one another and we both agreed that sometime we would be married. It was through her that I had my first contact with the Catholic faith. This is not to say that I eventually became a Catholic in order to marry her. Mollie always said that she would marry me, even if I was an Anglican clergyman, but the idea of conversion certainly became more attractive through my love of her. I had, however, to satisfy myself about the truth of Catholic teaching.

For a long time I had nurtured a growing dissatisfaction with the Church of England. Much as I loved its liturgy and music, it was plain then, and even plainer now, that it possessed no centre of authority: the bishops were not unanimous in their teaching, still less the parish clergy. One Sunday at Quatford, after serving at a communion service, I discovered that the vicar had left the remains of the consecrated Host on the altar. When I asked him what to do with it, he answered 'Oh, just bring it along and I will put it in a tin. We can use it again next week'. The priests at Cowley would have put it into the Tabernacle with great reverence. It was clear that contradictory teachings about the Sacrament were permitted. They could not both be right.

My studies at Oxford, added to the doctrinal shambles of Westcott House, had shown me that the Gospel as presented by the Church of England was not the Faith for which martyrs had suffered. One does not die for a probability. Fr. Ronald Knox aptly described the situation in his poem *Absolute and Abitofhell*.

When suave politeness, temp'ring bigot zeal,
corrected 'I believe' to 'one does feel'

A friend of mine who was about to be ordained replied to my question concerning belief in the Real Presence with the admission that he had never heard of it! This is not a theological treatise and I do not propose to go further into the matter. Suffice it to say that Christianity, being a religion not discovered by reason, but revealed by God, there must be some means by which that revelation can be preserved from corruption. The Catholic Church has always claimed to be that means. Therefore I should become a Catholic.

I did not reach this conclusion lightly, but read widely on both sides. The books which finally convinced me were Newman's *Apologia* and *Essay on Development*. I had now reached a turning point in my life: I must give up my training, abandon my career and join the forces.

The first thing I had to do was write to my father. It was the most difficult letter I had ever written, for I knew it would distress him; he had set his heart on my ordination and it was already arranged that in the summer of 1942 I should take my post as curate at St Peter's, Wolverhampton. As I expected, Father was mortified. He rushed up to Cambridge to see me and we spent a whole afternoon walking on the Backs and arguing. The arguments went round in circles; nothing either of us said could convince the other. With a heavy heart he returned to London and the bombs.

I promised that I would talk to a sensible Anglican clergyman and Father chose Canon Gillet, Principal of Chichester Theological College, now evacuated to Peterhouse. I kept my promise and had a long interview with him. I was surprised that the Canon produced no real arguments at all; he ended by telling me that I was suffering from Roman Fever and would soon grow out of it. Now at the age of seventy-seven, I am still suffering from it. When I told B.K., his reaction was very different. He told me to think very carefully and he would have me back at Westcott free of charge for one more term while I did so. He described to me the difference between an Anglican and a Roman priest: the Anglican clergyman was a gentlemanly amateur, while the Roman was a professional. If that was true in 1942, it most certainly is not so now. I finally left Westcott House in March 1942 after a tea with B.K. at which he gave me two boiled eggs. He told me that he always gave boiled eggs to students who became Roman Catholics. There must have been some deep significance attached to this, but I never discovered what it was.

I returned to Quatford. No more preaching now; I must simply find some work and wait to be called up. I passed A1 in my medical and was told that in due course I would be summoned to join the Royal Artillery. Meanwhile, I found a job with Mrs Phillips, the pork butcher in Bridgnorth. Her son was in the army and she had no one to help her. My daily task was to cut up large sides of pork into squares of about one third fat and two thirds lean; it was beautiful meat which came into the shop and I thought it a shame that it should all be made into sausages and pork pies. However, their quality was astonishingly high. While I boned and cut up the meat in the yard behind, I used to hear Mrs Phillips discussing me with her customers, or in hushed tones describing the details of her daughter's recent confinement. On Fridays I had to carry the pork pies on trays through the town to the bakery. My parents' grand friends would sometimes pass me by with astonished expressions on their faces. The Vicar of Astley Abbots, where I had preached the offending sermon, railed at me for having joined Mussolini's church; he must have thought I was a fifth columnist.

I also joined 'Dad's Army', the Home Guard. Its main task seemed to be the guarding of the railway tunnel, but I was never put on to that. I remember only one exercise, during which I was ordered to guard the vicarage at Quatford. Sitting on a stool by the front door all day, I read most of Barchester Towers.

Fr. Gilbey had arranged with Abbot Trafford that I should go to Downside Abbey to receive instruction. I had the most peculiar ideas of what to expect. Knowing that there was a famous organ there, I packed the complete organ works of Bach in an already heavy trunk. I quite expected the Abbot's car, complete with chauffeur, to meet me at Chilcompton station. When I finally arrived, the station was empty and I had to ask a porter the way to Downside. I left my trunks behind and trudged up a muddy footpath, from which I could see the Abbey tower. When I reached it, however, I could not find the gate; in fact it does not exist. Rather than search for it, I decided to break through the hedge. Having done this I found myself in the middle of a large patch of cauliflowers. I eventually discovered the front door and was admitted by the Guestmaster, Dom Ninian Fair. My instructor was to be Dom Hubert van Zeller, a housemaster in the school; tall and ascetic in appearance, he was spruce and elegant. I felt as if I was sitting at the feet of a most important peer. He had no knowledge or experience of the background from which I came; he was a traditional old English Catholic, belonging to a culture remote from anything I had encountered before. He took me through the penny catechism and, much better, lent me a host of books on Catholic history over the previous hundred years. During the pleasant succession of lessons, reading and attendance at Mass and the Office, I was sometimes asked to help Abbot Trafford with his war work. This consisted of hoeing the beans, which filled the cloister garth, or tending the Abbot's hens. I played the organ occasionally but never unpacked the organ works of Bach. There were daily walks with the young monks and I became very friendly with Brother Illtyd Trethowan and Brother Edward Cruise, both of whom had visited me at Westcott House. The grand finale of my visit was to witness Pontifical High Mass on Whit Sunday.

Pontifical High Mass these days hardly differs from any other sung Mass, but in those times before the 'changes' it was spectacular; two processions met in the Sanctuary, one accompanying the Prior issuing from the sacristy and the other with the Abbot, processing from the West door up the nave. The Abbot was dressed in his black 'cappa magna' with a long train supported by acolytes. Later on in the proceedings the Abbot, sitting on his throne in the Sanctuary, had most of his clothes changed: different coloured socks were brought, gaudy, slippers fitted to his feet, vestments changed and new mitres placed on his head. If one condemns these things as ridiculous, it should be remembered that they all symbolised the respect and devotion of the community towards its Head. They were designed to magnify the office, not the person who held it. It is this confusion of ideas which has done so much to reduce the appeal of religion to the emotions and to eviscerate the Mass of its mystique.

I was received into the Church on 24th May, 1942. After a general confession, conditional baptism (there was some uncertainty over the validity of my Anglican baptism) and official recantation of heresy, I became a Catholic. I have never regretted it.

Downside is the ideal place for a convert from Anglicanism to be received. The church itself resembles a Gothic cathedral; many of the monks are converts; they used to stand round the piano in the calefactory after dinner, while I played them the Stanford in B flat and C Magnificats. I transferred easily to my new life.

It was not always so on returning home. When a friend asked Newman whether he liked other Catholics, he answered that he knew very few and those he had seen he did not like. I felt the same. Before I left Downside, Abbot Trafford asked if I would think about joining the noviciate; if so, he could get me off military service. I thanked him but refused. I did not think I had a vocation and I wanted to go back to Mollie.

In early June I received my call-up papers and was ordered to report to Church Stretton.

# CHAPTER IX

❧

# *The Army*

It was strange beginning army life at Church Stretton. I was only twenty miles from home and the Carding Mill Valley, where we did our 'square bashing', had been the goal of many of our picnic expeditions in the past. Up and down we marched for hours every morning as far as the gate where my mother used to throw a penny to a small boy when he opened it. 'To the front salute – one two – one – two-one, two, three, one.' The life would have been intolerably boring, but in spite of the seemingly pointless existence I was leading, I was buoyed up by a sense of well-being. We lived in a small private hotel, from which all comforts had been removed; bare boards in every room and double-decker beds upstairs. For meals we paraded with our mess tins at a local warehouse. One Sunday I even managed to bicycle to Bridgnorth to spend the day with Mollie.

One day in July we were all put on a train to be taken to our proper training units. It was like a mystery trip; after we passed Bristol, I realised with a sinking heart that I was gradually journeying further and further from home. We finally landed up at Launceston in Cornwall with the 176 Army Field Regiment RA. We fired 25 pounder field guns and I was to be trained as an 'Ack', that is a technical assistant attached to an officer. One of our tasks was to work out data for the aiming and firing of the guns; for this we had to master logarithms. Although my contemporaries, mostly younger than I, seemed to deal with these without trouble, I found them extremely difficult. I had never reached logarithms at school and found to my alarm that as an Oxford graduate I was expected to know more than the rest. If they had asked me to sit down and write Latin hexameters, I should doubtless have been the brightest in the class.

We did gun-drill under the most foul-mouthed sergeant-major I ever met. In fact the army gave me my first experience of the four – and six – letter words which have been in increasing use ever since. I was not shocked by sexual expletives; they mean nothing and are simply inelegant ways of adorning a conversation. What did, and still does offend me, is the constant use of Our Lord's name as an expletive; it is even worse when blasphemous words are used, apparently without thought, until they have become a habit. I learnt my own lesson very sharply: one evening in our hut several of the men were telling shady stories, all of which raised a laugh. At length I decided to tell one myself: the result was electric; there was complete silence until someone said 'Well, Bevan, I never expected to hear a story like that from *you*'.

Part of our initiation into the Royal Artillery was to hear a lecture on the regimental motto from the regimental sergeant-major. 'Now this 'ere regimental motto is in Latin – see? It is UBIKE (= UBIQUE) QUO FAS ET GLORIA DUCUNT.' An unwarranted stress on the final syllable betrayed the fact that the RSM's thoughts were wandering from the subject.

The camp was at Scarne Cross, a small suburb a mile from the town. Launceston was a beautiful place and I made many friends, notably Sid and Hilda May at whose house I spent nearly all my free time. Hilda was a leading light in the local Methodist chapel and very keen on singing. Another musical friend was Bombardier Gerald Raper, a music graduate from Leeds, who was an able choir trainer. Between us we founded the Dunheved Choral Society, which gave a performance of Bach's Christmas Oratorio in December 1942. The concert was memorable for one reason; our tenor soloist was a young man from London whose parents had been parishioners of my father. I can always say with pride that I accompanied Peter Pears at one of his earliest concerts. The Mays were kindness itself; they even had Mollie to stay with them for a weekend. On this occasion we decided to become engaged. Apart from the need for a dispensation from the Church, there was no obstacle to our marriage; we were both earning, if that is what you could call my pay as a gunner and Mollie's as a student nurse in Wolverhampton. We might not survive the war – so why not?

Shortly after Christmas the whole regiment moved up to Hessle, a residential suburb of Hull. This was an improvement on Launceston for most of us; not for me, however, because, although we found plenty of Yorkshire hospitality from the inhabitants no one could replace the Mays. No more Nissen huts now; we were billeted in proper houses. I can remember little about our occupations during this time, except for one monster exercise on the moors around Fylingdales during which our shells set fire to a huge area. We drove away and left the fire, which, for all I know, is still burning. During our daily round of petty jobs I found it a help always to carry with me a piece of wood and a hammer. Bearing these signs of useful employment about my person, I was not likely to be stopped on my way to a quiet cup of coffee with friends. In the army one quickly learns how to 'swing the lead'.

As the time of my wedding approached. I discovered that, according to King's Regulations, I had to ask my CO's permission to be married. He was as surprised as I was to find this rule, but gave permission and I set off for London a few days before the date arranged. I arrived at King's Cross just as the last underground train was leaving; it was going the wrong way, but with the Inner Circle that hardly mattered; since I was going to Mollie's aunt to stay the night in Chelsea, my ticket was for Sloane Square; Mollie was already with her. When the train reached Aldgate we were all turned off, as it was going no further. I then had to walk through the black-out to Chelsea. These days I would not have gone far without being mugged, but in 1943 it was different; no one spoke to me except another soldier, who was going the same way and walked with me along the Embankment. I finally reached Aunt Margaret's at 3 am. She had stayed up for me, but for propriety's sake would not allow Mollie to come downstairs. We had to converse from opposite ends of the staircase. Next day my parents came down and with Basil Moss from Oxford days, who was best man, we stayed at the Goring Hotel at Victoria.

For some weeks beforehand we had been bombarded by photographers who wished to record the event. On February 10th it was raining hard. We were married at the Holy Redeemer Church, Chelsea, under a tarpaulin roof; the church had been bombed in the blitz. Fr. Cronin from Bridgnorth married us and we then descended to the crypt for the nuptial mass, said by Fr. Valentin, the parish priest. The men from Westminster Cathedral choir sang or, rather, wobbled, at the back, the boys having been evacuated to Cornwall. As we walked out from the west door, all the photographers but one had fled. No doubt the rain, coupled with my rather shabby gunner's uniform, had scared them off. We held the reception at the Royal Court Hotel, Sloane Square. No kind of wine was obtainable, so we had to make do with Pimm's No 1. I think everyone was glad to have even a taste of alcohol.

We had decided to begin our honeymoon at Launceston with the Mays. We bought first class tickets, as this was a special occasion, but even the first class carriages at Waterloo were packed. At last we found two seats in a compartment and sat down. Hardly had we done this than a pipsqueak of a second lieutenant, a very temporary gentleman indeed, demanded that I should give him my seat. I refused and even showed him my ticket. He then seemed mollified and went on his way.

Crackington Haven, where we spent the rest of our three-day honeymoon, was beautiful. It rained all the time and huge waves lashed the cliffs; but we did not mind. We had the whole hotel to ourselves; there we sat in the long evenings in the flickering shadows cast by oil lamps and a coal fire. There seemed to be unlimited food with Cornish cream at breakfast. During the short days we went for walks and came back dripping wet. On the way back to London in the train Mollie suddenly announced that she had swallowed her wedding ring. It was a joke, of course, but I had not yet learned the lesson that everything women say should be taken with a pinch of salt.

Although our honeymoon was short, we had the opportunity some three months later of resuming it at a hotel at Combe Martin, near Ilfracombe. There were no cars on the roads, private motoring having been abolished by petrol rationing, and we spent a week walking and travelling locally by bus. Returning to Hessle I conducted the local choral society, disinterred by Gerald Raper, in Haydn's Creation. Shortly afterwards we were moved again. This time it was further north to Gosforth Park racecourse, near Newcastle. We occupied premises previously, I presume, the abode of horses, but it was a pleasant place with countryside bordering our parade ground. At the gate of the estate was a village church, which had been taken over by the Catholics, where I played the organ for Mass. While I was at Gosforth a remarkable coincidence occurred; I was shaving at one of the outside wash basins when I looked beside me and there was Maurice! He had arrived the night before with his unit of signallers. We did not, however, see much of each other, as our routines were so different.

At this time periods of leave seemed to follow one another with frequency. I suppose the army was increasing at such a speed before the D Day invasion that the authorities did not know what to do with us. Mollie and I spent a week with my Mexborough cousins at Arden, near Helmsley, a visit described by Mollie in her autobiography *Against All Advice*. I returned to Gosforth and the persecution of Sergeant Dowdall, a Welshman who took great pleasure in giving me a bad time. Once, at Hessle, I was ordered to paint his motor bicycle. This I did, not sparing the engine which I deluged in its most secret recesses with red paint. It had to be revived by the REME engineers. When I left the unit, Sgt Dowdall somehow discovered Maurice and transferred his attentions to him.

I had decided to try for a commission, but before I could do this, I had to attend the War Office Selection Board. I was therefore summoned to

Spondon House, near Derby. The two days I suffered there left me
wondering what could be the point of the test. We were told that the
examiners were looking for 'officer material', the sort of people who
were natural leaders. We were given a battle exercise, during which,
naturally, everyone tried to be a leader; the field was full of cadets
shouting 'follow me, men'; no one else took the slightest notice, as they
were announcing the same message. I had to jump from a platform over
a twenty-foot drop and grab a hanging rope; that was unpleasant
enough, but the worst thing was vaulting over the horse in the gym. I
had never been able to do this but on that occasion hit the obstacle so
violently that I thought I had damaged all future chances of fatherhood.
When Maurice attended the same test some months later, the exam-
ining officer admitted that he did not think Jesus Christ was officer
material; Maurice failed to qualify but, to my eternal surprise, I passed.
As at Shrewsbury, I was given a stripe (unpaid) and was now a Lance
Bombardier. For many months afterwards Mollie addressed me as
'Bom'.

I began my training at a 'pre-OCTU' unit at Wrotham in Kent, but
managed to spend a day or two with Mollie, staying with Aunt Margaret at Seaford. Wrotham was a big camp built on top of a hill. We did
nothing there that I had not done before, but the theory was that we had
to do everything perfectly before we began to train as officers. At
weekends I used to walk down to Snodland station and take the train to
Rochester. There I would visit the bishop's palace and have lunch with
Bishop and Mrs Chavasse, whose sons had been with me at Shrewsbury; unfortunately they were all serving abroad at the time, but Mrs
Chavasse was very good to me.

After four or five weeks we all moved up to Catterick for officer
training. Of all places in the British Isles, I think Catterick is the worst.
Situated on top of the first hill between the Ural Mountains and the
Pennines, it is bombarded continuously by icy blasts from Russia. The
quarters themselves were by army standards reasonably civilised. Off
parade there was plenty to do and the large garrison Catholic church
was near my own lines. I made friends with the Finucane family, very
good Catholics, whose father was a retired Sergeant-Major. They even
had Mollie to stay for a week. I fear we must have been a nuisance to
them, but they never complained. On another visit I obtained a 48-hour
pass and we both stayed in a hotel in Richmond, the beautiful cobbled
town on the opposite hill. We were greatly embarrassed one evening:
while we were both saying our prayers a couple of officers burst into
the room – mistakenly, I hope – but withdrew hastily with awkward
giggles when they saw our kneeling figures.

At the tend of our course we had to attend a week's 'battle camp' in the Lake District. We climbed Helvellyn and ran down again; we ran for miles and miles. One of my companions actually passed out but no one took any notice; he soon recovered. Our next diversion was a visit to the firing ranges at Trawsfynnydd (or 'Trousers' as it was colloquially called) in Merioneth. We dropped tons of high explosive on the moors and pounded wooden tanks to pieces on the beach at Harlech. We were now considered to be trained and ready for our commissions. We had an extraordinary battery commander, whose name I cannot now remember. He was very small and dapper and was known as 'Twinkletoes'. Cadet Sloan, a communist, wrote and asked him for permission to spend a weekend with Sir George Trevelyan. The letter was returned with SNOB written across it. Before our passing-out parade he gave us a lecture, which contained the following gem: 'You will, after this parade, be officers and – some of you for the first time – gentlemen. Of one point I wish to remind you: no gentleman ever takes a cigarette, lights it and puts it behind his ear.' On the next day I put up my one pip and took the train for Wolverhampton. I have always tried to remember never to put a cigarette behind my ear.

I spent the first part of my officer's career travelling about the country on training courses. We were really waiting in a queue to join the invasion of France, but the battle did not begin for a few more months.

My first posting was to Consett, a grim town in Durham, dominated by an enormous steel works. Another officer and I were billeted in a sleazy pub. There was little to do, the other officers in the unit not seeming to know of our existence. I did visit my old regiment at Gosforth Park; I need not have bothered. I expected to meet my old friends, but they were embarrassed by my uniform and even the sergeant-major looked the other way; such is the English class system.

Shortly afterwards, after a day or two snatched with Mollie, I was sent on an anti-aircraft course at Newtown, Montgomeryshire. This was to have a great effect on my future: the parish priest was Fr. Roscoe Beddoes. He was a convert from the Church of England and an Oxford man. He had a colourful past and had been known throughout the university as an eccentric character. Six years older than I, he had been there in the early Thirties, before the Oxford of Evelyn Waugh and *Brideshead Revisited* had quite been replaced by earnest purveyors of Socialist politics. He had money and expensive tastes; it was not that he was self-indulgent, but he bought the best of everything. His shoes were hand made and his clothes of the finest quality, exquisitely tailored. At Oxford he had dressed like Count Dracula, but as a Catholic priest he had simplified his garb to a long black cloak with an extremely tall biretta on his head. In summer he sported a white alpaca coat with Panama hat. In the town he behaved like a country squire among his tenants, walking down the High Street with a mincing step, greeting with courtly bows any passing acquaintance. The Catholic chapel was at Newtown Hall, the residence of Bobby Arbuthnot. The pious ladies of the parish used to complain about the scanty clothing and bare legs of his children sunbathing on the lawn outside the church on Sundays.

Several times a week I would spend the evening with Roscoe. Together we devised a plan whereby he would build a new church and, if I returned from the war, a school. Mollie's mother had fallen victim to terminal cancer (the harrowing story of her illness and death is told in Mollie's book) and it was known that her house near Bridgnorth would in any case have to be surrendered to a farm worker. Roscoe very generously agreed to have Mollie and her brother, Rupert, in his house if the worst happened. It did, and after I had been posted abroad they moved in, Mollie acting as housekeeper. Priests' housekeepers were supposed to be of 'canonical age', certainly over forty, and Mollie was only twenty. The townsfolk gossiped, of course, but Roscoe was not interested in women except for purely social reasons.

All this, however, was in the future. I stayed only four weeks in Newtown, during which I slept in a tent in the gardens of Dolerw Hall, which eight years later was to be our school. I was moved on to other scenes including two visits to Salisbury plain where at Larkhill I watched the aeroplanes flying over to open the Normandy invasion.

A course on motor transport brought me to Rhyl in North Wales. The summer season was in full swing and there were the usual amusements on the beach, including Punch and Judy shows and donkeys. Mollie spent a weekend there and thoroughly enjoyed it. I have, however, one bad memory of this course: the motorcycles. I had never ridden one of these machines before and one outing at Wrotham had done nothing to calm my nerves. I had just avoided by half an inch running into a shop window on a busy Saturday in Dartford. At Rhyl we all lined up along the sea-front ready to ride into the mountains. The signal was given to start our engines; of course I could not start mine: I stood kicking the pedal while everyone else took off with ease. Finally I was left alone on the promenade frantically kicking the starter. I looked round and found that I was quite alone and began to think that I would put my machine away and have a quiet day on the beach. But no, the sergeant-major had counted the names and found me absent. He came back, started my engine and led me at break-neck speed up the narrow lanes until we reached a steep hill with a river running at its foot. We all had to spend the day riding our cycles through deep water, rushing up the hill and down again. By the end of the day I could do anything with a motor cycle except start it. I have never ridden one since.

We had an extremely uncomfortable anti-tank course at Lydd in Kent. We were not in the village but slept in empty houses on the marshes behind Dungeness. Here we were in the direct path of the flying bombs or 'doodlebugs', which flew over night and day making a hideous roar. The roar did not matter; it was when it stopped that we started worrying; that meant that the bomb was about to descend, as many did before they reached London. And one of them might have our name written on it.

My final posting was to Otterburn in Northumberland, a wild and remote spot in the Cheviot Hills. This was a holding unit from which drafts were sent to France. After about a week I was told to prepare myself to go on embarkation leave; I was to go, with several friends who had been with me since Wrotham days, not to France, but to India.

I arrived at Bridgnorth to find that my mother-in-law was worse and not expected to live long. Generously, Mollie's Aunt Margaret rented a house at Morville, just outside the town, where she could stay with Mollie and me. We were near enough to visit Mollie's mother every day; it was a sad time, especially for Mollie who would be left to look after her family while I was at the other end of the world, at least for the foreseeable future. Before embarkation we both spent a few days at Watford with Dr and Mrs Cox, parents of an Oxford friend who was later tragically drowned while bathing in Cornwall. At length the order came for me to report to Watford Station; Mollie went home at the same time. I got into the train and, as it drew out of the station saw her on the other platform. We waved and that was the last we saw of each other for nearly two years.

Mollie returned to her old house; she was not to move to Newtown until November. Her mother died on September 17th, but I did not know this until I reached India.

Meanwhile my train sped north-westwards until we were shunted into Liverpool docks. There, waiting for us, was the P & O liner 'Stratheden'. Before embarking we had to make our wills; I thought the quayside was an unusual place for this. We had two-tiered beds in a large cabin, housing about twenty officers. The men slept further down in hammocks; they were squashed together in a most uncomfortable manner and later in the voyage were insufferably hot. Officers, on the other hand, had a much better time. We had a large recreation room with armchairs, a wireless and a grand piano. We ate in the first class dining room at tables for four or five. For some reason this part of the ship did not seem to have been put on to a war footing: we were waited on by white-coated stewards and given hotel food.

That night we sailed up past the Isle of Man and anchored in the Clyde opposite Greenock. The whole of the Firth was teeming with ships of every conceivable size; a contrast, this, to when I visited it forty years later; there were then no ships at all. In the Clyde our convoy mustered and a day or two later we sailed past Ailsa Craig into the Atlantic. As we passed the Foyle a flotilla of destroyers steamed out to escort us. We sailed out into mid-Atlantic and zig-zagged southwards, to avoid German submarines. Fortunately they left us in peace, but it took us two weeks to reach Gibraltar. Here the weather brightened up and became warmer as we went eastwards; it was wonderful to lean over the rail and watch the flying fish spring up out of the waves. We stopped at Port Said but were not allowed to leave the ship. On again through the Suez canal and Red Sea to Aden; most of the passengers spent their time watching the obscene antics of the Arabs lining the shore. The heat was stifling; no wonder the Children of Israel rebelled. After a month's voyage we arrived at last in Bombay.

No sooner had we boarded the train than it was invaded by a crowd of boys asking for 'baksheesh'. They clung on to the train and peered in at every window. Some of them were selling Indian silver and various knick-knacks, probably made in Birmingham; it was surprising to see the ease with which some of the soldiers parted with their money. The biggest sales were of bananas. None of us had seen a banana for four years, so that the men pounced on them. After eating six bananas in succession they began to feel ill; the after-effects lasted for several days.

After a few hours journey up into the mountains, we left the train at Deolali. This was an enormous camp from which thousands of troops were sent all over India. We had few military occupations and except for some desultory Urdu lessons, were free to wander round the town. Everyone was buying silk underwear to send home. It was cheap, but when my parcel reached Mollie, she could not fit the shirt over her shoulder nor drag the knickers above her knees. We went one day to Nasik, not to see the birthplace of Gandhi, but to inspect a factory which produced Indian whisky, rum, gin and brandy. At the top of the warehouse was an enormous vat (made in Wolverhampton) full of molasses; on the surface was an assortment of rats and various creeping things. The liquid was passed down a pipe which branched out into various tubes; it had by then turned into a watery-looking substance which eventually landed at a desk manned by a babu who added the appropriate colour. No wonder that these drinks all had the same taste, and were quite different from European spirits.

By now I had become acclimatised; Deolali, being high up, was not desperately hot, and I had become used to the insects which buzzed round me every evening and the bugs and creepy-crawlies which landed on my book or drowned themselves in my gin. I was ordered to travel alone to Secunderabad, near Hyderabad. Hyderabad is one of the chief cities in India and I would dearly have loved to visit it. It was, however, out of bounds; Secunderabad was nothing but a suburb built for British troops and containing only bungalows. It was my misfortune to have been in the British army, which was always kept apart from the country, its culture and its inhabitants. Unless I was travelling, I had to eat conventional English food cooked by English cooks; if the cooks decided to go native and produce a curry, it tasted of nothing and the rice was a dank, squidgy mess. More often we had tins of bully beef and 'soya links', foul sausages made of American beans. The only time I ever had a decent curry was on the Calcutta-Delhi express, where a friendly Indian businessman ordered one to be handed in at the window at a station. By the time I had finished it the sweat was rolling down my face.

At Secunderabad I joined the 86th Medium Regiment, which was being converted from 6.6" howitzers to 25 pounder field guns. As a field gunner I was told that my job was to advise the officers on the gunnery. Of course no one wanted my advice; they all knew far more than I did. Military activities produced nothing memorable and the only event worth recording was my visit with a friend to the local cinema. We were received with smiles and graciousness by the manager, who escorted us to a box, where we sat in dignified splendour, sipping whisky brought by an obsequious bearer. From downstairs came a continuous crunching sound, which I found to be monkey-nuts; everyone was eating them and the husks were ankle deep on the floor.

A move just before Christmas took us up to Ranchi, a small town in the hills of Chotanagpur, about 300 miles west of Calcutta. This area had never been Hindu or Muslim: the inhabitants were aboriginals. Until the British came, the natives no clothes, but the wolf-whistles of the 'brutal and licentious soldiery' soon compelled them to change their ideas. We were truly in the wilds. The country was a broad plateau guarded by steep valleys leading down to the plains. The weather was cool in summer and in winter there was even an occasional frost.

Apart from the usual day-to-day routine, our job was to practise firing on the ranges. These were large tracts of land populated by small villages of aboriginals, who scratched a living from the soil, mainly by growing paddy. Before we went out with the guns, the police used to clear out all the inhabitants, who were paid eight annas each for their trouble. Many of them left the old people behind, in the hope that we might drop a shell on them. Of course we never aimed to kill people nor destroy their homes, but there was always the odd officer who would drop rounds in the wrong place. On one shoot, not taken by me, thank goodness, a 25 pounder landed in a tree around which several Indians were skinning a goat, which they joined in an untimely end. When the shooting was over, all the inhabitants would be sitting round the edges of the target area, waiting to go home. The Indian police were there, laden with fruit and vegetables which they had doubtless extorted from the terrified victims.

The Chotanagpur area was strongly Catholic. Untrammelled by Hinduism or Islam, the local people received the Faith with eagerness. The first Jesuit missionaries lived in hen houses, but the mission prospered so rapidly that by the time I arrived, Ranchi boasted a bishop, cathedral, seminary, several convents and schools of all types. The Belgian Jesuits, who were in charge, were men of great holiness and devotion. I never heard one of them make an uncharitable remark about any of his colleagues. Not so the one English Jesuit who lived there. He complained about everyone; this is, of course, a peculiarly British failing as the Romans discovered; the Britons quarrelled so much amongst themselves that they fell an easy prey to their conquerors. I made many friends amongst the Belgians and was twice invited to go on holiday at their seminary in the Himalayas at Kurseong, near Darjeeling.

I shall never forget those journeys to Kurseong and they come to me even now in my dreams. After a hot sticky night in a sleeping car from Calcutta, I was faced with a wall of mountains rearing up ahead; at Siliguri, at the foot of these hills, I changed on to a narrow gauge railway. I was usually the only passenger in the observation car, which had glass all round and a bar at the end. There followed the most stupendous journey; higher and higher, zig-zagging up the mountain we climbed. Kurseong was about 6,000 feet up, and from it one could see the distant snows of Kanchenjunga. At the station I was dismayed to find that my heavy cases were to be carried to the college up a steep flight of seventy-five steps by women. When I tried to insist on carrying them myself, they became quite angry. They walked with my boxes on their heads and as we passed through the village I saw the male population seated by the roadside, smoking and playing cards.

At the college I was given a private retreat by one of the fathers and there were walks and picnics. I was warned against leeches, which cling to one's legs and suck the blood, and against the dreaded King cobra which will attack on sight. I learnt at Kurseong how to accompany plainchant. In many ways the life lived there reminded me of Downside. The fathers ate breakfast in silence, drinking coffee out of large bowls. At tiffin (lunch) and dinner they were read to. Afternoon tea consisted of tea in bowls, slices of bread and huge basins of sugar cane to spread over it. Not a diet for diabetics.

Among the students was Graham Langford. He was preparing to serve as a priest on the Bengal mission. Unfortunately, when British rule ceased, all British clergy were sent home. Fr. Langford went to the diocese of Clifton and forty years later I met him again when he was chaplain and I organist at All Hallows, Cranmore.

Back at Ranchi life went on as usual. I was appointed assistant adjutant and one of my tasks was to keep the regimental accounts. I had never seen an account book before, let alone kept one. I was given about fifteen minutes instruction, of which I understood nothing, and left with the 'baby'. Things went wrong very soon and I discovered eventually that the difference between the bank statement and my account book was 10,000 rupees. Hurried conferences followed, to which I was not invited, and I thought that I was due at least for a court-martial. Nothing, however, happened except that I was relieved of the accounts.

In May 1945 I had my first experience of the monsoon, which occurs at different times in different districts of India. Black clouds appear on the horizon; they pass over without dropping anything for about a week, but each day becomes darker than its predecessor. Finally the whole sky breaks out into an enormous thunderstorm with rain descending in sheets such as you never see in England. Hailstones as big as marbles fall on your head, so that it is necessary to wear a tin helmet. Lightning flashes from all points at once and the thunder is continuous. This goes on for about four days. The lulls between the storms gradually grow longer, but it is July before the weather becomes settled. The effect on the landscape is miraculous: fields which were hard baked and cracked suddenly push forth rice shoots; dried river-beds become raging torrents; insects produce wings, fly round the lights and drop into your soup.

About five hundred yards from our camp was a native village, separated from us by a large patch of tall grass. This village provided a hunting ground for various gunners who needed to satisfy their sexual appetites with the young female inhabitants, known as 'Bibbys'. Apart from moral considerations, this practice was considered dangerous to health and steps were taken to prevent it. One night I was ordered to patrol the grass patch and arrest offenders. I crouched in the long grass for what seemed hours, when a heavy hand fell on my shoulder with the order 'Stand up that man!' I stood and was embarrassed to see one of my fellow officers who thought I was an erring gunner in quest of a Bibby.

A few months after our arrival in Ranchi the 86 Medium Regiment was disbanded and I was posted to 160 Field Regiment in the same area. We had a comfortable Officers' Mess in a small compound which contained the mess itself, surrounded by straw huts (bashas) in which we slept four to a hut. In the middle of the compound stood a mango tree, under which the Commanding Officer would sit by himself drinking whisky from about four o'clock onwards. He drank a bottle a day and it was my job, re-appointed as assistant adjutant, to keep him supplied. As this necessitated occasional trips to Calcutta, I did not mind.

Since I was in charge of drinks and extras, such as Christmas dinner, for the whole regiment, I hit upon the idea of buying pork for Christmas 1945. The Jesuits at Ranchi kept European pigs; the Indian variety were small, black and not very appetizing. Accordingly I bespoke four piglets during the summer and watched them grow. When the time for killing arrived the CO advised me to clear them with the medical officer. Without inspecting them, he immediately pronounced them to be unfit for human consumption; this was simply because they had been bought from 'natives' (Belgians!). He ordered the pigs, which had already been killed, to be burnt. I gave them to the Jesuits, and I hope they had a good Christmas.

Earlier in the year, in August, I was sent on a secret mission. One of our batteries had been sent to occupy a position on the coast just south of Madras, in preparation for the invasion of Malaya. I had first to travel to Poona to collect a new type of gun-sight, which, it was hoped, would increase the accuracy of our firing and the discomfiture of the Japanese. I had to cross India three times, once to Poona and then to Madras and finally to Ranchi again. The gun-sights were handed to me in a sack, which I stowed under my bunk in the train. On reaching Madras I was invited to patronise the establishment of Madame Mitchell, but virtuously declined and stayed at the Officers' Rest House. Next day, after a hair-raising journey in an Indian post office van, I found our battery. I returned and went to bed as it was late. There was a noisy dance going on next door, but I went to sleep. Suddenly I was awakened by clapping and cheering, which went on for such a long time that I thought something serious had happened. Indeed it had; news had just come in that the atomic bomb had been dropped and the Japanese had surrendered. The men posted on the coast were, I heard, disappointed. I was told later, however, that the Japanese in Malaya had not heard of the surrender, knew our troops were coming and were quite ready to give them an unfriendly reception.

After this the 160 Field Regiment either faded away or was sent off on other duties. I, however, was posted to 85 Medium Regiment. No sooner had I changed my billets than an order came through that I had qualified for LIAP, Leave for Indian Army Personnel. This involved a return air journey home with a month's leave. About a week before Christmas I was told to report to the Officers' Rest Camp at Ranchi, preparatory to travelling to Calcutta. I had hoped to be home for Christmas and Mollie was expecting me. I should have known what would happen. A new order came through saying that my journey was to be deferred. I stayed in the Rest Camp, but the days went by and nothing happened.

Meanwhile I had to resign myself to staying in Ranchi over Christmas. I sent Mollie a telegram, addressed to 'Newtown, Wales, UK'. The babu who took the cable promptly sent it to New South Wales, Australia, so that Mollie continued to expect me for Christmas. She spent the whole of Christmas Day meeting trains at Newtown, finally returning in tears to a Christmas dinner with Fr. Beddoes and her brother.

Not knowing of Mollie's predicament, I made the best of things at Ranchi. In fact this Christmas gave me one of the great experiences of my life. I was asked to play the services in Ranchi Cathedral. There was no organ, only a harmonium, but at midnight Mass I accompanied some four thousand aboriginals, many of whom had tramped through the jungle for three days to get there. A large choir sang the *Missa de Angelis*. But even better was the morning Mass: this was for the East African division, at that time stationed in Ranchi. The nave was packed with African soldiers and with me in the gallery was a choir of 150 more, who sang the Proper in perfect plainchant. Never have I been so deeply impressed by the singing of the Chant.

Eventually I set off for home. From Calcutta we flew across India in a Dakota to Karachi. I had never flown before and was somewhat alarmed to see oil emerging from one of the engines. However, we did not crash. At Karachi we were warned that we would be flying in superannuated bombers, of which two out of every five were unfit for service. We did not mind; we were going home. We stayed overnight at Tel-Aviv but were not allowed to leave the airport because there were troubles in Jerusalem. The most I saw of the Holy Land was the long ridge of the hills of Judaea in the distance. Next day we flew to Libya; again we were confined to camp. For the last leg of the journey we flew in a De Havilland York, a proper passenger plane. It was good to be able to see out of the windows. On reaching home, bad weather forced us to

Wales, where we had a few narrow misses with mountains suddenly rearing up on all sides. Eventually we landed at Shawbury, only thirty miles from Newtown. The Army, of course, made us travel by train to London, where I stayed the night with Aunt Margaret. At last I appeared at the door of 'The Cross' where Mollie was living in Newtown, and we were reunited after eighteen months of separation.

The month's leave sped by: we visited my parents at Quatford and with Fr. Beddoes made our first plans for the founding of the school. We decided to buy a commodious house near the new church, called 'Crescent House'. This had been the sergeants' mess and had useful outbuildings which could be used as classrooms. We used the money which Mollie's mother had left her, plus a sum from Fr. Beddoes, who in the end signed away the whole of his fortune to the school and church. The latter was to be a disused warehouse, which was already being converted while I was on leave in February 1946. Mollie had started a small choir of local children to sing in the church at Newtown Hall. All of these eventually became pupils of our school.

I managed to secure a short extension of my leave to take my MA at Oxford. My father came to the ceremony where a grateful university applauded my former successes with the examiners. Finally Mollie and I went to Aunt Margaret's in Chelsea for the last few days before my departure.

I was whisked away from England on a dark morning in freezing fog. We landed at Marseilles for lunch in brilliant sunshine and were waited on by pretty girls with flowers in their hair. By evening we were in Egypt. There were pyramids behind the camp; with a friend I decided to explore them by night under a full moon. Each pyramid had an entrance with a passage sloping down to an iron grill, behind which was a tomb. There was no other way out and when we turned to leave, there, blocking our path, was a jackal. I had heard that these beasts could be particularly vicious when thwarted. I prayed hard to St Francis, who ordered it to go away; we did the same. Next day the final lap of the journey brought me to Karachi, Calcutta and Ranchi.

The war being over, there seemed to be nothing to do in the 85th Medium Regiment. A few desultory exercises, designed to prevent the Russians from invading Bengal, were organised, but the Army began to have other ideas: we must all go to school. I was put in charge of education for the regiment and was hard put to it to find teachers who knew anything. We had one mathematics teacher and he had to work hard, because his was about the only subject anyone wanted to learn. I did not think that Latin and Greek would be in demand, so I confined myself to religious instruction (Pope and all) and current affairs. The men learnt very little. The only benefit I received was promotion to the rank of Captain, which pleased not only me but also the bank manager.

Demobilisation was in progress and there were many farewells to be made in Ranchi: to the Jesuits and to one of their native students, Cyril Tirkey, a youth of about nineteen who said that I reminded him of King George VI and implored me to take him home with me, where he would be my faithful servant for life. I often wonder how he would have fared, had I been able to take him.

In September 1946 we sailed in the Georgic, a large troop ship which was filled to bursting point. As on the Stratheden two years earlier, the men lived in heat and discomfort. So did we, except in the dining room. As before, the authorities had seemingly preserved a peacetime regime in this department and we were eating five-course breakfasts, starting with cereal and continuing with bloaters (!), bacon and eggs, toast and marmalade and fruit. There was an admirable Anglican chaplain on board who taught everyone folk songs and dancing, at which he was an expert. He had all the lower decks dancing as well. I was not so happy with the Catholic chaplain, who spent most of the voyage at the whisky bottle and boasted that he could say Mass in ten minutes. Landing at Liverpool we travelled somewhere up north to draw an extraordinary collection of 'de-mob' clothes; then to London and on home, where Mollie was already expecting our first child.

I had had an easy war. I never saw either a German or a Jap, nor even a shot fired in anger. Two years separation from my wife was no more, and considerably less, than many others had suffered; and unlike the writers of many heart-rending letters which I had to censor in India, Mollie had never run off with the postman nor slept with the milkman. I sometimes suspect that in return for my comparatively pleasant life something very nasty is being prepared for me in this world or the next.

# CHAPTER X

❧

# *Newtown*

When I arrived at Newtown, Mollie had changed. In the six months since I had left her at the end of my leave she had grown up from childhood. She had always been a devoted wife and companion but still a young girl, utterly dependent on me; now she was a woman, sturdily self-reliant and beginning to show those qualities of shrewdness and confidence which were to be so characteristic of her, marking her out as a mother-confessor to so many who were in trouble.

At first I felt like a stranger in the house, a house which was not mine; I noticed that Mollie relied on Fr. Beddoes more than on me. This was natural, since in my absence she had come to regard him as a kind of substitute for her mother. I suppose many returning soldiers had the same problem, but much of the blame lay with me. For years I had lived in an institution; not only the army but school and university. I did not have to worry about the next meal, let alone cook it and wash it up, and I had become the slave of an easy-going routine. After breakfast on my first day I sat down and reached for the paper. This was quietly removed and I was directed to the sink. For many weeks after that I spent my time cleaning, turning out cupboards and gradually learning how to run a house. Mollie had given up housekeeping for Fr. Beddoes, her place being taken by a pleasant middle-aged woman, Mrs Mackness; but we often had meals together at which Roscoe would say grace: 'Bless us O Lord and this extraordinary dish cooked by Mrs Mackness, through Jesus Christ Our Lord – Amen' or 'We thank thee Lord for this burnt offering so cleverly provided by Mollie'.

It is the custom nowadays for fathers to be present at the births of their children. This must be the wife's idea, as I am sure that the midwives would far rather manage without their help. Mollie always protested that I was the last person she wanted at that juncture and that

I would be much better employed making tea for her to drink afterwards. John Francis Xavier was born on 15th December 1946 in the Newtown hospital; we called him Francis Xavier in thanksgiving for my safe return from India. Aunt Dorothy (Miss Bates that was) came to help when Mollie returned from hospital, but the doctor had made her stay there through Christmas. We had to eat our Christmas dinner without her in the warehouse which was soon to be the new church. In those days mothers were kept in bed for a long time after childbirth.

Shortly afterwards we moved into Crescent House, the old sergeants' mess, which had been bought with Mollie's money. We lived for several months on my army gratuity. The winter of 1947 was the coldest of the century. Snow fell a few days after Christmas and stayed until mid-March. In addition to the snow the temperatures never rose above freezing for three months. Those were the days of rationing far more severe than during the war. The coal ration was absurdly small and the heating arrangements at Crescent House were prehistoric. We had to cook on a paraffin stove and used so much electric current keeping the kitchen warm for the baby that the manager of the electricity board came to remonstrate. These were the early days of Attlee's Labour administration when every facet of our daily lives was ruled by little dictators who sprang up in every local office. Our particular hate presided over the fuel office; he always had a good fire burning there, so one day, after our application had been turned down, Fr. Beddoes took a packet of sandwiches to the fuel office, planted himself in front of the fire and announced that he was staying there until he obtained his coal. He did.

One day the roof valley of the house filled with snow which then melted underneath and began to leak through the ceilings. Roscoe and I had to go up and shovel the snow into the garden. Unfortunately the pitch of the roof was so steep that we could not throw it over. The solution was to break a skylight, throw the snow on to a blanket below and tip it out of the window! I had by now become conversant with the art of interior decoration and spent most of my time on a ladder, preparing classrooms and dormitories.

When the thaw came at last, we drove, partly by hired car and partly with my parents, through the floods for a week at Quatford. There we collected large supplies of crockery, knives, forks and other necessaries. At an auction in Bridgnorth I bought six double-decker army beds. These were cut in half and put in the dormitories. They were not very comfortable, but we were at least making a start. We were not disturbed by any bureaucratic meddlers. I shudder to think how we would have fared today. We bought a number of wash stands at another auction;

these we made into desks by filling the holes with circular pieces of wood. The furnishings were ramshackle, but they worked. It was years before we could afford new desks and many boys passed their examinations on the wash stands.

During the spring I had an offer from Mrs Clark, who had been in charge of our canteen at Ranchi; her niece, Angela Brooke-Fox, who had lost her husband during the war, wished to come and help us, bringing her four-year-old son, Charles. Mrs Clark herself would come when the school opened and act as cook. Angela became School Matron and stayed with us many years, eventually marrying Jim O'Dwyer, the school doctor. Charles was at our school, St Mary's and St Benedict's, for the whole of my time as Headmaster; after Douai and Oxford he became a doctor.

We went to see Bishop Petit enthroned in the Catholic church at Llandudno, where several years before the parish priest had died of starvation; most of his flock were summer visitors and in winter the parish was deserted; everyone forgot about the priest. Bishop Petit was always kind to Mollie and me, but with his clergy, especially Fr. Beddoes, it was a different story. In the old days before Vatican II I used to think that at their consecration bishops were given the special grace of rudeness. Nowadays they tend to be polite and gracious. Bishop Petit's wrath was reserved for Fr. Beddoes, whom he bullied mercilessly and in public. On one occasion Roscoe was nervously attempting to open a conversation with his Lordship: 'I hear, my Lord, that Franciscans are soon coming to Llanidloes.' 'Oh, indeed,' was the reply, 'well, the best thing you can do, Father Beddoes, is to keep your ears open and your mouth shut.' The Bishop told us to have as many children as God sent us and gave us, via Roscoe, a cheque for fifty pounds. Roscoe put it in the church funds.

The new church was solemnly blessed by the Bishop in June 1947. The building itself was not prepossessing, simply a rectangular brick warehouse, but Roscoe had furnished it with exquisite taste; he once said that it reminded him of a nobleman's private chapel, an idea which was completely characteristic of him. Since we intended that much care would be taken with the music, the new school being a choir school to serve the church, a brand new Walker two-manual organ was installed in the west gallery. Before the opening ceremony, Roscoe insisted that the Bishop wore a tall Roman mitre; the suggestion did not meet with approval; the Bishop preferred the usual tea-cosy. He gave way, however, with good grace. Roscoe would have nothing in his church which was not thoroughly Italian: statues, furniture and vestments. On great occasions he would process up to the altar stiff with cloth of gold, tears streaming down his face.

By this time the school had already opened. We began the summer term with one boarder, Robin Lindsay-Smith, five day pupils of just over eleven and about six infants. Mollie taught the infants and the rest were divided between myself and Brian Pontet, an ex-RAF man, who later joined the staff of Ladycross, Seaford. With such a large staff-pupil ratio the children received close attention. Our fees were ludicrously low: £40 per term for boarders and £10 for day pupils. This was less than my parents had paid for me in 1927; no wonder we were in perpetual trouble with money.

By September we were able to organise ourselves better: one notable addition to the staff was Anne Brennan-Smith, usually known as Mona, who came from Ireland to take over the kindergarten. This quickly became the fastest developing part of the school, for parents soon realised that if they wanted their children to read and write early, Mona was the person to teach them. She stayed longer than I did. Another new teacher was David Woodard, an old Oxford friend of mine and a recent convert. He was not really cut out for teaching and quickly lost patience. His shouting and screaming in class could be heard in the street and must have caused him much nervous stress. The children, however, loved it and were devoted to him. He became a priest and died in the 1980s, while parish priest of Burnham.

One of our troubles with staff was money: we could not pay them more than a pittance; £150 per annum was the norm, less than my father's curates were paid in the Thirties. The result was that our choice lay between two kinds of teachers, those who were full of missionary zeal (very rare) and those who were either mad or otherwise un-employable; of the latter we had a good supply, but they did not stay long. As for Mollie and me, we received no pay at all. I used to teach private piano pupils on Saturday mornings in order to earn a few pounds.

The senior part of the school grew more slowly but after about two years non-Catholic day children began to come in, which helped with the finances. All Catholic schools are faced with the problem of re-ligious instruction for non-Catholics. It is easy to admit too many, so that they begin to outnumber the Catholics and the nature of the school is changed. I have seen this happen in some other Catholic schools and have sometimes wondered why they appear in the Catholic Directory. We had religious instruction from 9 am to 9.40 am. Non-Catholics who did not wish to attend this class arrived at 9.30. Catholic day children who could not afford them paid no fees. At first I tried to charge them for school dinners but gave up after vain efforts to extract any money from them. 'I'll pay you next Friday without fail' was the weekly reply to my overtures. I knew their feelings myself when, some years later, I was trying to bring up a family of eight children on a pre-Burnham scale salary.

Oddly enough the parents who paid no money whatsoever were the most vociferous in their complaints. I once received a complaint from one of our Catholic parents that both the Principal (Fr. Beddoes) and the Headmaster (myself) were Oxford MAs. They were Irish and, I suppose, saw in us the sinister influence of the Ascendancy.

Our boarders were increased in number by the arrival of the Poles. These were all sons of officers of the Polish army in exile. Much to Fr. Beddoes' delight, they came mostly from aristocratic families. Our first task was to teach them English, which they all learnt surprisingly quickly; one boy, who spoke only Polish when he arrived, passed the Common Entrance into Stonyhurst after two years, gaining 97% in Latin. Working with them were a few local boys and girls; one of those boys reached O level in Latin and Greek. His parents took him away to work on the railway, where he became the only British Rail ticket collector who could read Xenophon.

A red-letter day in our lives – it must have been March 1949 – was the arrival of Josef Nowoscynski. He had been batman to one of our Polish parents and came as gardener-handyman. He took over all the manual side of the school work. Before that Mr Henry (later Fr. David Henry of the London Oratory) and I used to feed the chickens and ducks every morning. Josef took over all this and established a sort of personal kingdom with which none of us dared to interfere. He never mastered the English language, but spoke a sort of patois which only we could understand. His Polish was highly spiced with language so colourful that I had complaints from the parents. Sometimes he asked my advice, especially on gardening problems. I showed him how to plant asparagus, but he immediately planted them his own way and they died. 'Mr Bevan, I not plant it this sparagy more; all die. Sparagy no good.' When Rachel was born in 1952, Josef was her godfather. At her baptism, when the salt was placed on her tongue, she made such an extraordinary face that Fr. Beddoes laughed. Josef was shocked; 'In Polonia priest not laugh.' There were other Polish workers in Newtown and every Friday they gathered in Josef's room for a party at which spirits were consumed neat in enormous quantities. They never made a sound but slowly drank themselves into a stupor. Josef never suffered any after-effects and was always up early the next morning.

One of our aims in founding St Mary's and St Benedict's was to provide a choir to sing the liturgy in the new church. I decided that the difficulties of singing polyphony, in fact any harmonised music regularly, were too great to be worth tackling: we should depend too much on outside help by unreliable singers. I therefore decided to confine ourselves to plainchant. We already had the nucleus of a choir in the children Mollie had trained at the old church. With the addition of others from the school we collected a choir of twelve singers. With daily practice in school hours they became familiar with the chant and were eventually able to sing a full Mass with Proper, Vespers on Sundays and Compline on five weekdays. Occasionally we joined other singers for a concert and we gave one memorable one with the Deller Consort, of which Maurice was a member.

I still retained some of my Anglican illusions about the Catholic Church; I imagined that I only had to provide good music and everyone would be falling over to hear it. With this in mind, I asked the Administrator of the Pro-Cathedral at Shrewsbury if he would like us to come and sing Compline one day. He said the he would be delighted. After a train journey to Shrewsbury we walked through the town, carrying our robes until we reached the church. By now, I thought, the crowds would be flocking in. When we entered the building, it was completely empty except for a cleaner with mop and bucket. I was directed to the clergy house next door. The bell was answered by a dishevelled curate, who looked as if he had been listening to the races all afternoon. He looked mystified, scratched his head and asked 'And what can I do for you, sir?' When I replied that we had come to sing Compline, he looked as if he thought I was a lunatic and directed us back to the church: 'You just carry on, then, and I will join you when I'm ready, but don't go waiting for me.' So off we went, sang Compline in an empty church and left for home. On another occasion we did encounter crowds: we visited Bala, at that time much in the limelight as a shrine to Our Lady of Fatima, to sing Vespers. As we processed into the church in our choir robes, we had to squeeze our way through a double line of waiting pilgrims; the church, however, was empty and remained so while we sang. After we had left the building, the pilgrims all crowded in for Benediction. I suppose it would be no better now, unless we each carried a guitar instead of a Liber Usualis, but those were the supposedly palmy days before Vatican II, when the Latin liturgy is said to have flourished; I never noticed it. The Catholic Church in England has shown, since the Reformation, no interest in music. In the old days everyone wanted cheap, sentimental hymns; now they want uninspiring English words set to music which is trivial, boring and evocative of the 'pop' world. How can such music raise the mind to God? I vowed that I would do what I could to improve the situation. This could only be done by instructing the young at school, and this is what I set out to do.

In 1949 I was asked to conduct the Newtown Operatic Society in a performance of *The Mikado*. This was followed by the conductorship of the Newtown, and then the Welshpool, choral society. By this means I was able to make many friends in the locality and thus further the interests of the school. Singing is the national pastime in Wales and it was most enjoyable training the choirs; they were never afraid of singing and one never had any of the cringing, apologetic approach to the music which choral conductors find in England. The notes were not always correct, but at least one could hear them. I once conducted Handel's Messiah at Newtown. After careful rehearsal through the winter, I arranged a full practice in the local cinema on the afternoon of the performance. Imagine my astonishment when I was suddenly faced with a choir which I had never seen before; it was twice the normal size, for every regular singer had brought a friend. 'I hope you don't mind, but I couldn't resist a good sing, so I came along.' They muddled their way through just like the chapel choirs from which they came.

When Mona Smith arrived to take over the Kindergarten, Mollie became cook. She stayed in that post until we left in 1953; the kitchen became the meeting place for everyone, staff and friends, when they wanted a rest and change from their routine. In the midst of all their troubles Mollie managed to cook wonderful meals. One boy, whose parents had invited him to lunch at the Bear Hotel, asked if he might join them after lunch, so that he could have his meal at school. On another occasion the river overflowed into the gasworks, so that we had no way of cooking the school lunch. Mollie persuaded Josef to collect all the wood he could find and light a fire in the garden. Lunch for sixty was ready at one o'clock and everyone ate outside. Photographers came up from the town and we were all in the newspapers.

Our second baby was a daughter, Mary. I had always wanted a girl and was thereafter very close to her. I was sometimes accused of favouring her above the others; I always tried not to, but it was difficult. After her baptism John was sitting in his high chair entertaining the guests with a recital of hymns, which he sang accurately in a loud, clear voice. I thought this remarkable in a child of less than two. It was repeated by many of his younger brothers and sisters, the beginning of the Family Choir which was to be.

John, however, did not always sing. He went to bed at six o'clock, and from then until exactly eight o'clock he would scream his head off. He suffered badly from asthma, but there was nothing asthmatic about this performance. Our next-door neighbour, Mrs Richards, must have thought we were beating him, for she came round in a furious temper and accused us of maltreating him; to me she said 'Call yourself a BA? You're nothing but a B.F.'. Gwen was born in 1949; unlike Mary, who was fair, Gwen was very dark with brown eyes, like her mother's mother; 'This one has come down from the hills' said the nurse who delivered her. The Welsh are great poets. Three more Bevan babies were born while we were at Newtown. David was a sturdy little boy, much loved by Josef, whom he followed everywhere saying the only word he knew, which was 'Ba'. In Herodotus's histories there is a story of how an Asian king wished to discover the first word spoken by babies; it transpired that this word was 'Bara', meaning 'bread'. Perhaps David was simply imitating his forefathers. Rachel was the next: she had a difficult birth and from then onwards fought us throughout her childhood; she refused to eat, screamed through meals and did everything she could to annoy us. She grew up to be strong-willed and, to any who opposed her, formidable. Finally, just before we moved, came Tony; no problems with his birth, but Rachel bullied him mercilessly when he was small. He was probably the most naturally gifted of all our musical children.

Life was made easier for us by the arrival of Tony Sutkaitis, or 'Big' Tony, as he was later called, to distinguish him from our own Tony. He was a friend of Rupert's at the seminary at Osterley, where they were both studying. Big Tony had escaped from Lithuania, first from the Russians, who sent him to forced labour, and then from the Germans. He had walked across Europe living on berries and what he could beg, until he reached British lines in France. He was sent to a camp in England. Finally becoming a student priest, he had nowhere to spend his holidays, so Rupert brought him to us. At first he was shy and Rupert advised us to leave him alone and keep the children away. After a few days he was seen playing with them. 'Why did you tell them to keep away? I love children'. From then onwards he was their inseparable companion and played with them all day. He came every holidays, even when he had given up his studies and gone into an insurance firm in London.

We must now go back a year or two. Crescent House was gradually becoming too small for our school and in 1949 a large house came on the market, Dolerw Hall, previously the property of the Pryce-Jones family. It was a large Victorian house standing amid spacious meadows, which led down to the river bank. The fields were not for sale, but I was assured that one of them could be used for games. It was an ideal place. No sooner had we made an offer than the Council came in with a compulsory purchase order. They wanted it for offices. This was no doubt an anti-Catholic ploy, since the Council was well housed already. In those days, there was much anti-Catholic opposition from the chapels. Nowadays much of that has died down, not so much because of increased religious toleration, but through indifference to any kind of religion. We never attempted to hide ourselves and would hold our Corpus Christi processions through the streets from church to school. During one of these I suffered for the Faith when a small boy catapulted a stone and hit me on the nose, causing my martyr's blood to be spattered over my Westminster Hymnal.

The dispute with the Council was settled by an appeal which was heard in the town. Roscoe had employed a KC friend from London, who made mincemeat of the opposition, and the case was declared in our favour. We immediately organised a Mass of thanksgiving and procession.

There was now room for all and our next task was to secure recognition by the Ministry of Education as an efficient school. This would mean that, among other benefits, our children could travel on the school buses. We were at this time having trouble in finding a mathematics teacher. Luckily I discovered that Algy Haughton, later an English master at Ampleforth, had opened a new preparatory school at Newcastle Court, near Presteigne; he had an Austrian baroness, Miss Scholley, who seemed to have the right qualifications, and we arranged a Box and Cox plan whereby she should spend two days a week teaching maths with us, while I taught Latin at Newcastle Court. How the inspectors took this I cannot now remember; perhaps they had gone before it happened. The prospect of having a baroness on the staff delighted Father Beddoes, who treated her with studied politeness: 'Headmaster, kindly pour out a fresh cup of tea for the baroness'. Miss Scholley had a sense of humour and was greatly amused.

The inspection, preparatory to recognition, was a gruelling affair. An educational fad at that time was that Latin should be easy for children; in other words grammar was out, stories of life in ancient Rome were in. It was the thin end of the wedge, which was to lead to the evisceration of classical studies, so that they became divorced from classical language. This produced that particularly inept subject of classical civilisation, in other words, Latin without *Amo*. Two generations have since grown up ignorant of grammar and thus without any foundation on which to build their studies. Most other subjects have suffered from the same doctrines and made the British the worst-educated people in Europe.

After spending three days with us and vainly attempting to persuade Mona Smith to crawl about on the floor with the infants, the inspectors departed. A few weeks later came the news that we were now officially recognised. Another procession and Mass of thanksgiving, followed by a party at which the French teacher laced all the drinks with gin. I need not dwell on the results.

We now had about seventy pupils in the school and I was beginning to feel more confident as Headmaster. It was time to take stock and decide in which direction we should go. The boarders were no problem; we simply had to prepare them to pass the Common Entrance into their public schools, and in this we were very successful. The problem of the day pupils was different: few of them were destined for other schools. Some passed the 'eleven plus' and went on to grammar schools, but for others there was no future unless we could take them on to the GCE at O level. I decided to do this. Had I stayed on, we might have succeeded better, but the unexpected happened.

For some time I had not worked happily with Roscoe Beddoes. His outlook was totally different to mine: he did not seem interested in the children's education but thought all the time about the 'shop window'. Quite rightly he liked the school premises to look tidy, but he took no interest in the pupils as individuals; in fact I think he regarded them as a nuisance. He wanted Dolerw Hall to be a Gentleman's Residence – with him as the gentleman. One year, when we returned unexpectedly from an abortive summer holiday, we found Roscoe installed in the house, entertaining a company of relations and friends who were not at all pleased to see us. He had a habit of speaking to the parents contemptuously of Mollie and me; 'those two children', he would say. This was unacceptable when, as sometimes happened, people would complain to him about something I had done. Finally he began to be sarcastic about my growing family: 'Your children will soon outnumber the pupils' he would complain, or 'I don't see why I should have to keep your vast family.' This when I was still paid no salary.

I still, however, had no serious thoughts of a change until the summer holiday of 1952 when we received a visit from Dom Illtyd Trethowan of Downside. He had been walking in mid-Wales and stayed a night on the way. During the evening Mollie and I both voiced our misgivings about our relationship with Roscoe and he asked me whether I would like a change. I replied that I would certainly consider it. Then he enquired whether I thought I could run the music in a school. I hesitantly answered that I thought I could and no more was said.

Three months later a letter arrived from Dom Wilfrid Passmore, the Head Master, asking whether I would be interested in the Directorship of Music at Downside and inviting me to an interview. Such an offer exceeded my wildest dreams and both Mollie and I went to the interview, she mainly to see what they were offering in the way of a house. I then received a formal offer of the post at a salary of £640 per annum with a house. I thought that these were riches indeed, but then I had never earned a salary before. The house was semi-detached with three small bedrooms overlooking a busy main road. It had a garden, but nothing like Dolerw, and we had six children. I was by now, however, so anxious to leave Newtown, that these considerations were mere details. Roscoe seemed to take on a new lease of life when he heard that I was going and began plans to take over the headmastership.

Before we left, Josef and his co-worker, Wiktor Kulas, invited me down to a pub for a drink. I innocently thought that all they had in mind was a few pints of beer. I was sadly mistaken: on arrival at the pub I found that it was to be a real Polish orgy. A tumbler was placed before me and a bottle of Martell three-star brandy. They filled my glass, wished me 'Prost' and drained theirs at one gulp. I plodded slowly on until my tumbler was empty. Then, horror of horrors, it was replenished. On we went until I had demolished three tumblers of neat brandy. I was on the verge of unconsciousness, but my two friends hauled me up and frog-marched me back to school. Mollie was dreadfully alarmed and walked me round the grounds for an hour; I could have died, I was told, and certainly spent the next day with a monumental hang-over. Josef and Wiktor were perfectly sober.

The prizes that term were distributed by the Head Master of Downside and everyone went away. Mollie and I remained to await the birth of Tony, which took place a fortnight later without complications. Day after day we sat in the big school room, our furniture piled around us, looking at the river and the hills beyond. I read aloud to Mollie. This was the beginning of a daily practice throughout the rest of our lives together: over the years we read the whole of Jane Austen, The Brontës, George Eliot, Dickens, Trollope, Hardy as well as diaries and biographies.

In mid-August, the furniture having gone ahead, we drove away in two cars: Rupert took Mollie, Tony, David and Rachel in his Morris Minor, while in my Austin 14 (1931) I drove the older children with 'Big' Tony. Leaving the Welsh hills behind us, I braced myself for the Mendips; could the two compete?

# CHAPTER XI

## Downside Abbey (1)

I had arranged for the house in Stratton-on-the-Fosse to be unlocked when Mollie arrived, and for the electric current to be switched on. She arrived but the front door was locked; no one knew where the key was; in fact no one knew who we were. I arrived soon afterwards to find that the Bursar was away and had left no instructions. I cannot remember when I finally found the key, but neither the gas nor the electricity had been connected and we had nothing to cook with. At least the furniture had been installed, so we could sit down. I should never have arrived in August; everyone was away, including the monks. We settled down, however, and heaved a sigh of relief: at last we were alone; no more staff at every meal; we could now sit together undisturbed after the children had gone to bed; we were a family. The first day I decided to celebrate by driving to Wells and buying a whole Dover sole each for Mollie and me. We had no money, but that did not matter. We put the car away and for more than two years relied on buses or trains. For half-a-crown I could buy a day return from Chilcompton to Bath, Green Park, and it saved money to shop there on Saturday mornings. I often bought a leg of mutton (7d per pound) which would last much of the week and was extremely good. Why can we not get mutton now? Years later, when we reared our own sheep, we kept one until it was a year and a half old; the meat was superb.

In spite of having six children in a small house, we found St Anselm's very comfortable, but could not last long there. The garden was small and faced a busy main road; it would be difficult when the children were older. John was the only one at school and he used to go across the road to St Benedict's, the village school. It was run by Servite nuns, who became great friends of ours, but it was a rough place, quite different from what John was used to. During the summer our children played happily in the back garden, or stood by the front gate chatting up the villagers waiting at the bus stop. Only one neighbour called on us at first: Neville Watts lived opposite, with his wife Clare. They both made us feel at home. Neville was the 'Mr Chips' of Downside, having taught classics in the school since before the Great War. He took me for long walks in the Mendips. On one of these we walked to the Ebbor Rocks, then down into Wells. As we entered the city we passed a cricket match; Neville watched for some minutes, sighed and said 'Ah well; if the Germans had played cricket there would have been no war'. A splendidly British observation.

Mollie was much occupied with housework. We had no washing machine; everything had to be done by hand. For cooking we had electricity and gas, the latter being home-made, supplied from the abbey gasworks, which stood outside the present art room. The gas supply was temperamental and one never knew whether to expect an explosion or a shower of soot over the stove. Although it was dismantled some thirty years ago, the site of the gasometer still smells of gas. We had a coke stove to heat the kitchen and water. Fortunately household work was never a chore for Mollie; she enjoyed it and considered it as part of her vocation in life to run the house smoothly. She became a skilled cook, mainly by continually having to make meals out of nothing, which is the supreme test. On the other hand Mollie never went out. She liked me to take her to Bath or Wells occasionally, but the social life which my job often entailed did not attract her in any way. She hated coming to school functions, either at Downside or at other schools which the children attended in later years. Consequently I had to provide the liaison between home and school. It became the normal practice for me to take the children to the dentist, the cinema or on a visit to their grandparents while Mollie stayed at home with the babies. When during the summer holidays I organised a day's outing to Beer, in Devonshire, Mollie preferred to stay at home; she did come once and avowed that the seaside was so horrible that she would never go again. Mollie had no wish to drive, so that shopping had to be done by me; she always said that the menu would have been more economical, though less interesting, if she had bought the food. I enjoyed shopping. All this time our marriage was happy and secure. It was simply the way Mollie preferred, and we were content.

My first term began in mid-September. I had given much thought to the way in which I should approach my work. One thing was certain: I had a free hand and was working on virgin soil. My predecessor, who, I understand, saw his post advertised in the paper before he had been given notice, was an excellent pianist. There were, in consequence, some good pianists in the school but nothing else. There was neither choir nor orchestra; about six boys learnt the violin, two the cello and a handful wind instruments, all taught by the same master, John Buckley. John was an amazingly clever musician; trained at Leipzig as a concert pianist before the war, he had learnt from his father, a bandmaster in New Zealand, to play every wind instrument in the band. He also had a way with boys which enabled them to learn quickly and willingly. We decided to give up the old drum and fife band, with its uninspiring music; we sold the fifes in Bristol and bought brass instruments. The military band quickly gained in expertise until in 1957 it carried off first prize in the Mid-Somerset festival.

Strings were a bigger problem. It was obvious that not much would be done by the teachers already there, so I got rid of them and engaged Bill Smethurst, who had been a peripatic violin teacher in mid-Wales and possessed the right temperament and attitude to get the string section off the ground. We had many volunteer learners but nowhere to play. I allowed them to use my own room, which was tucked away in a tower, surrounded by bathrooms. About three violinists could practise in each bathroom, while the cellists sat on the lavatory.

Before I came the boys gave no concerts at all. The annual music making was confined to the 'Carol Concert', an event which occurred in the wooden gymnasium; the singers came up from Midsomer Norton but few boys took part. The Head Master had ordered me before I came to remedy that situation. During my first term I formed a choral society; I had to teach them the difference between treble, alto, tenor and bass, but they soon understood the idea and sang six carols in harmony at the end of term.

Music in the school was in a far worse state than at Shrewsbury in 1932. This was partly due to the attitude of certain members of the monastic community. I was told at my interview that music was at Downside the Cinderella of the arts. I was supposed to be the fairy godmother, but it was an uphill task. At the beginning of my first term, I decided to call on the housemaster of the Junior House, to enquire about the use of his boys as trebles in the Choral Society. After I had sat down in his room he said: 'Before we discuss anything, I think I had better tell you that I dislike music masters on principle; nothing personal, of course.' He reluctantly allowed me to have his boys, but persisted in his unfriendly attitude to me.

The music accommodation was absurdly primitive. The room, from which I was expected to manage the department, was stuck at the top of a tower, up four flights of stairs. The rest of the teaching took place in two shabby wooden huts, turning out of the gym which had been erected as a temporary building in 1909. There were no practice rooms; pianos were distributed among the classrooms, so that it was impossible for anyone to practise in privacy; these pianos were subjected to rough treatment, which ranged from having cups of coffee poured into them to providing a hiding place for illicit supplies of alcohol. In fact, the idea of practice being necessary if one wished to progress in playing an instrument did not seem to have penetrated the minds of the authorities. It was difficult to gain support from housemasters in dealing with boys who persistently neglected their practice, or even failed to turn up for their lessons. At many times in my career I had to go round the classrooms rooting out pupils who cheerfully imagined that they were free to miss lessons if they wished.

The musical scene was surveyed from the touch-line by a musician of European reputation, Dom Gregory Murray. He had at one time been Director of Music in the school, but his main interests did not lie in that direction and he was busy with other responsibilities. Nevertheless he was a tremendous help to me in acting as accompanist to the Choral Society; he turned up loyally every week and played continuo on the organ at all our performances for about twelve years. He was, however, a strange man, perpetually at war within himself over the claims of his monastic vocation over his music. When musicians visited the school, they would often ask to see Dom Gregory. If successful they were sometimes puzzled to be received curtly and given the impression that he was totally uninterested. After about 1968 he withdrew entirely from the school musical scene, but he was always good to me.

The school was closely wedded to the music of Sullivan and a performance of *Trial by Jury* had been arranged for my first term before I even arrived. An amusing event occurred in connection with this: dressed in my dinner jacket I made a ceremonial entrance into the orchestral pit, took my bow and turned round: there was no orchestra; I had forgotten to summon them from the Green room. I crept out and fetched them; no one seemed to notice; I daresay they thought that this was some arcane ceremony peculiar to musicians, who were all mad anyway.

I soon discovered that I was expected to perform a Gilbert and Sullivan opera every year. I knew that, had I agreed to the plan, with our resources as they then were, nothing else would ever be performed. I gave way for one more performance, *The Mikado*, in June 1954, but put my foot down about the future. Fortunately the Lord intervened by burning down the gymnasium. It was fire from heaven. I did, however, manage to stage a performance by the Choral Society of Handel's *Acis and Galatea*, in the summer. By then I felt that we had at least our feet on the ladder.

Every school Director of Music has to make up his mind on one particular point regarding public performances. His duty is to give everyone in the school the chance to become interested in music and, if possible, to perform in some way. On the other hand he has a duty to those already interested, especially the few who are gifted, to cater for their needs. The two duties do not mix easily. If you shepherd hordes of musically illiterate children into your choir, the quality of the performance cannot fail to be poor. You can help matters by importing a large number of experienced singers, if obtainable; but the children then feel that they are being taken over and lose interest. I generally used only volunteers for the choir, adding perhaps a small number of grown-up singers to give them confidence. The boys then felt that they had got to learn their music properly and give performances in which they could take a pride. Modern audiences are so accustomed to high quality performances on radio or gramophone, that they do not easily tolerate the second rate and are slow to make allowances for school standards. They should not need to.

The idea of oratorio performances was quite strange to Downside in the early 1950s. No one had even heard of Handel's Messiah. When after the fire I decided to perform it, most accepted the news with resignation, but one monk spoke virulently against such a 'beastly Protestant work'. After practices had begun it was not long before boys were humming the choruses as they went about the school. I decided that every boy should have the chance to sing in a Messiah at least once during his school days. I kept to this until the mid Sixties, by which time tastes had become more sophisticated and it was no longer necessary.

Before I was appointed to the Downside post, I had been told that I would play the organ for all school services in the Abbey Church. In fact it was that side of my duties which attracted me most and caused me to accept the post. I was sadly disappointed to find on arrival that the Head Master had changed his mind and it was to be thirteen years before I played for the school Mass. Perhaps he was right: it was not an easy position to fill; too many people would be breathing down my neck.

At the end of the 1954 school year the Bursar arranged for us to move to a larger house. There was nothing available on the Downside property, so he bought Downside Lodge, Chilcompton. This was a seventeenth century stone-built house of ample proportions, standing in a spacious garden containing out-houses. It was exactly what we wanted. The house was in bad repair, but the Bursar patched it up and we moved in in August. Our furniture looked rather silly in the large rooms, but my parents managed to send us a lorry load from Quatford; best of all, Cousin May, a Molesworth relation who lived in Bath, sent us another lorry filled with beautiful furniture, carpets and eighteenth century looking-glasses from her mother's house in Edward Street. It had all been in store. She sent us these beautiful things not on loan but as a present; many of them are still with me now.

The garden now occupied much of my spare time. We were able to grow our own vegetables and in that realm were almost self-support-ing. We started to keep poultry and even branched out into guinea-fowl. They were, however, of doubtful benefit; I think we managed to eat two; the rest flew into trees, nested in the fields and were taken by foxes. Early on we acquired a goat; Mollie had a way of pasteurising the milk which took all the 'goaty' taste out of it and the children drank it readily. Later on we branched out into pigs; we never tried to breed them, but used to buy two weaners together and fatten them in a shed, feeding them with our own leavings together with some pig meal. It was a wonderfully economical way of producing meat, although I am sure that the army medical officer in India would have ordered them to be burnt.

In January 1955 Rupert, my fourth son and seventh child was born. By this time my parents had grown tired of lecturing me on the size of my family. By worldly standards we were foolhardy; my income, even by the standards of the early Fifties, was barely enough for two chil-dren. As far as work was concerned, the brunt fell upon Mollie. I was out every morning but usually came home in the afternoons and read to her; in the evenings I often had to be at school until 9.30 pm, but on those days when I was free, I put the children to bed. Mollie loved children; there were no 'mistakes' or unwanted children in our family. The hardest work was when there were four under five, but that did not last long; the older ones, especially the girls began to take a hand, and although the numbers grew, the work became easier. We did make life more comfortable for all of us by insisting on certain standards of behaviour: first, obedience was insisted on, for without it nothing could be done. I am not afraid of a good smacking for a small child; it is a much more humane punishment than long drawn-out household or garden labours. On the whole our children had received all the smacks they needed by the time they were five. Quarrelling was another vice which we abhorred. I seldom bothered to umpire between two sides in a fight; better to punish both. On the other hand we did not allow ourselves to get into moods or harbour grudges against the children. I never forgot the time – I was about twelve – I misguidedly told my father that Miss Bates, our governess, had said that she did not like him. I knew that the feeling was mutual between them. My father was angry with her and she in turn with me; instead of telling me off, she put on a 'mood' whenever I was near and, when we passed in the passage would whisper in my ear 'cad'. As Miss Bates doubtless intended, I was made miserable over this for days. I vowed not to do that to my family. My children grew up to be very affectionate towards each other as well as towards us; when they went out into the world, say to London, they always kept in touch with one another and met as often as possible. In my retirement they visit me regularly.

Of course a large family can have its disadvantages. It develops a strong tribal sense and outsiders meeting its members for the first time can find it a gruelling experience. Several of my sons-in-law have described their embarrassment at being scrutinised by innumerable pairs of critical eyes. Some of my son's wives have found the pressure of family ties hard to bear.

After our move to Downside Lodge, we decided to have done with school altogether and teach the children at home. The time of special-ised education had not yet arrived, as they were still young. We sent for the PNEU syllabus and affiliated ourselves to that organisation. We secured the help of a retired school teacher in the village, Mrs Dyke, for mathematics and geography, two subjects which Mollie could not manage, but Mollie taught them everything else, including music. It was in these music classes, mainly singing, that she discovered that the children could sing in parts without trouble. We entered them for the folk-song competition at the Mid-Somerset Festival, where their small size and extreme youth attracted much notice, but not, alas, the prize. Later, when the Bristol Professor of Music, Dr Willis Grant, visited us, five of the children sang him a three-part motet by Palestrina. From these small beginnings sprung the Bevan Family Choir.

To assist my flagging finances I secured, in September 1954, a part-time post at All Hallows Preparatory School, Cranmore. I planned to visit them during the afternoons, when Downside were playing games. I stayed there for forty years. My task was to teach a few piano pupils, train the Chapel Choir and take recorder classes. There were two of these each week which included the whole school. When I entered for my first class, I saw and heard, horror of horrors, fifty boys all blowing descant recorders. After a few introductory lessons, being a confirmed élitist, I sorted out the best players and put them in a room by them-selves. The rest was pandemonium and after twenty minutes I used to gather them together for 'musical appreciation', that is gramophone records with commentary. I have never taught class recorder playing since then, and hope I never shall.

In those days preparatory school masters were not chosen according to the rigid criteria which now obtain. I do not suppose that All Hallows had a single qualified teacher in 1954. The senior masters were experienced, but the younger ones were either ex public schoolboys waiting to begin their careers or a few specimens of that class of eccentrics whom we should nowadays call unemployable. I had employed several of these at St Mary's and recognised the type. A few masters, however, possessed real character: one of these was James Douglas, who remained my close friend for the rest of my life. A former Anglican clergyman, he had recently become a Catholic and was marking time at All Hallows before deciding on his future. He left after two years to study for the priesthood in which he pursued an unusual career. After leaving the Beda in Rome, he wished to devote himself to the Byzantine rite, but was first sent to Canada, where he proved an *enfant terrible* to the authorities. He returned to Rome for further studies and worked in Milan for the mission to Russia. A long spell in a German parish brought him to early retirement in France, where we meet annually. I think he can preach in at least five languages. Another of my colleagues in those early days was Mallowan, brother-in-law of Agatha Christie, the detective writer. 'I have taught in most of the prep-schools in England' he once remarked 'I leave applying for a job until the very last moment in September, because I know that by then headmasters will be desperate and will take anyone, provided he hasn't just come out of prison.'

The Headmaster, Francis Dix, was an unforgettable character. He spent most of his time teaching Latin and Greek in a stentorian voice; his grammar tests could be heard throughout the building; in fact I once arrived at school to hear this noise going on inside his study, where Dix was stamping and bawling at an unfortunate boy. 'What is the matter?' I asked a throng of wondering boys. 'Oh, Sir, Duncan is doing his Harrow scholarship and Mr Dix is helping him.'

My salary at All Hallows was a princely £16 3s 4d per month, but it helped. I was able to found a tradition of church music, much of which managed to survive the disastrous changes of the Sixties.

To return to Downside. Under Fr. Wilfrid Passmore the aims of the school grew ever more academic. All able boys were expected to sit for entrance scholarships to Oxford or Cambridge and the middle and late Fifties were marked with great success in this direction. I quickly realised that if music was to gain respect in the establishment, I must aim for academic success. Accordingly I prepared courses for GCE O and A level candidates parallel to those in other subjects. I could not have fulfilled my ambitions without divine intervention; this came in the person of Jerome Roche, a very intelligent boy who arrived in 1954 with a modern languages scholarship to Downside. In the normal course of events he would have passed through the language department and ended with a university award. Jerome was, however, an exceptionally able musician even at the age of thirteen: he could read complicated piano music at sight and when I taught him the organ he soon outstripped his teacher. I realised that this was 'he that should come' and set about steering him towards a music career, an idea which he found attractive. After a few years and many battles with the school authorities I sent him up to St John's College, Cambridge, for the scholarship examination. I knew that I was 'sticking my neck out', for if he failed, I should never again be taken seriously. A week later came the news that Jerome had won the top music award at St John's. I do not think I can claim much credit for his success, since Jerome was so able that he would have gained a scholarship even if taught by one of the prep school unemployables. His future fulfilled his early promise: after gaining a First at Cambridge, he became a PhD and one of the foremost authorities on music in Italy in the early 17th century. He then became a Senior Lecturer at Durham University.

Contemporary with Jerome was Nicolas Kynaston. He had previously been a chorister at Westminster Cathedral, where he had received organ lessons. This presented me with a problem: apart from the Abbey organ there was no suitable instrument in the school. For a while I used the organ in the village church, which was utterly inadequate. Requests to use the Abbey organ were met with firm refusal; finally I arranged for the use of an organ in the Methodist church at Chilcompton. Both Roche and Kynaston used to spend afternoons there and there can be no doubt that this arrangement contributed greatly to their progress. Nicolas left the school early for Rome, where he studied under Germani, finally gaining a national and European reputation as a recitalist.

A Benedictine school is not quite like any other. The monastic community not only runs the school but forms its Governing Body, of which the Abbot is chairman. All the key posts are in the hands of the monks: Head Master, Bursar and housemasters. Although there had always been lay masters, in earlier days they were few in number and low in status. By the time I arrived, although their numbers were perforce increasing, little effort was made to increase their share in running the school; lay masters even received invitations to attend

Prize Day, much of which they had themselves organised. It was not until the Sixties that this situation was remedied.

Fr. Wilfrid ran the school like a prep school. He was in sole charge and there was little or no delegation to housemasters. If I took a party of boys to an evening concert, I had to report their return to the Head Master in person. Corporal punishment was normal. On one occasion when the cast of *The Mikado* had been caught smoking, he beat them all, fifty boys before lunch and another fifty afterwards. Fortunately for the victims, Fr. Wilfrid's eyesight was poor and the blows often landed on the chair. When caning is carried to this extreme it becomes a joke. In Marryat's *Mr Midshipman Easy* the doctor recommended beating as a cure for pride. True as that may be, I agree with Dr Butler, the great Headmaster of Shrewsbury, who remarked: 'I hold flogging to be for small boys the best and for big ones the worst punishment'.

Masters were not spared Fr. Wilfrid's wrath: every morning he would be seen standing in the main hall watching to see if anyone arrived late. One master, who had habitually transgressed in this way, entered his classroom to find the Head Master sitting at a desk with the pupils. Every morning we looked nervously at the common room table, where a white envelope addressed to one individual betokened dismissal. In other ways Fr. Wilfrid was an attractive personality: he always had time to talk and never looked at the clock; he made you feel that you were the very person he wished to converse with and you left his study with a feeling of elation. This lasted until you discovered that he had just spoken to another master and said the very opposite of what he had just said to you. 'Divide et Impera' was his motto. Of one thing one could be certain: in any dispute with a member of the Community, he always supported a lay master.

The newly formed string section of the orchestra soon blossomed forth. Smethurst used to go from boy to boy tuning the violins before the programme began; 'Why does Smethurst go round winding up the violins?' asked Fr. Wilfrid. The resulting music was at first wildly discordant, but it was a beginning. In one of these early concerts we produced a small wind band to play a composition by one of the monks, Dom Alphege Shebbeare. Dom Alphege had an embarrassing habit of taking a step forward at every sentence of a conversation. Anyone who was in his way had to step backwards. On this occasion while conducting the players, he behaved in the same way; they soon had to rise from their chairs and walk backwards as they played. By the end of the piece the musicians were cowering in a corner while Dom Alphege stood over them wildly waving his baton. The Head Master laughed so much that I thought he would have a heart attack.

Another light-hearted programme was Leopold Mozart's Hunting Symphony. During the last movement guns are directed to be fired. I borrowed two rifles from the Corps and two boys, dressed in tails, carried them into the orchestra. Unfortunately the blank cartridges which they fired made more noise than the composer intended, nor was it easy to restrict the shots to the exact points indicated on the score. The result was a riot: the audience stood up and cheered, monks put their hands over their ears and the room was full of reeking cordite.

In the summer of 1957 I was invited to take a choir from Downside to Liverpool to sing at the re-dedication of St Mary's, Highfield St., a Downside church recently repaired after bomb damage. We did the whole journey in style. The Pines Express stopped at Chilcompton and we travelled in a special coach with meals laid on. At Liverpool we had a large hotel at our disposal. Of the church celebrations I can remember little, except that Dom Gregory Murray played an electronic organ and we sang a Mozart Mass. The whole enterprise was undertaken with a lavishness which would be unthinkable now.

# CHAPTER XII

&

# *Downside Lodge*

At Downside Lodge the family school, under Mollie, progressed satis-
factorily, but the time was approaching when the task of teaching the
children had to be entrusted to an experienced person who could give
them the time they needed. Events at St Mary's, Newtown, solved our
problem. Fr. Beddoes had taken charge of the school when I left, but
had appointed a new headmaster to work under him. The new man
stood the strain for two terms and then died. Roscoe reverted to direct
rule and staggered on for a year or two, but he was no schoolmaster and
eventually began to look about for a purchaser for the school and
buildings. This he found in the form of the Holy Child nuns at Mayfield,
who were anxious to start a mission school in a poor area, which
Newtown certainly was. Accordingly the nuns took over, closed the
boarding school and conducted a highly successful day school, which is
still running.

Mona Smith was therefore looking for another post and decided to
come and help us by teaching the children. We were not able to pay her
much, but she generously agreed on a sum which was considerably less
than what I would have had to pay in school fees. She stayed for three
years, by which time the older children were ready for more advanced
education.

Meanwhile Cicely was born in February 1956 at home. The day
before her birth I had to go to Bristol and there bought for 15/-, a
great extravagance, a bottle of Clos de Vougeot which we drank
together that evening. Cicely has always been one of the healthiest of
our children.

In that same year we had the offer of a month's holiday in Ireland.
The parents of Webster Wilson, a colleague of mine who was later to
become Headmaster of the Oratory School, offered us the free loan of

their cottage on the beach at Rosscarbery, Co Cork. The journey there was horrific, the other travellers resenting the size of our family. On the Irish boat, however, we were made welcome; an obvious contrast between a Protestant and a Catholic country. Once there we had the most wonderful holiday I can remember. The children were absolutely free to wander where they liked, except into the sea. On the first day I was offered a large salmon trout for sixpence. We had no difficulties with catering. Cicely, only six months old, spent most of her time in a drawer. The others played on the beach or went fishing.

We returned to Downside Lodge to find mushrooms growing out of the walls and that curious dank smell which comes from ruins. It was only the heat from our Aga which kept the building standing. Financially we went from one crisis to another, until eventually trades-men began to call and demand their money. My old bank manager in Bridgnorth had been generous with overdrafts, but then a new Pharoah arose in Egypt, who refused further advances. I decided to approach Fr. Wilfrid, who gave me a lump sum to be deducted monthly out of my pay cheque. I drew the money from the Bursar, £200 in cash, took it home and showed the notes to the children; we all threw them about the room in joy at being temporarily solvent.

I have never been very good at economising and we certainly had to be careful. Our kind and understanding butcher, Mr Frank Shearn, used to scout the countryside for bargains, which he would bring up weekly in his van. Our most frequent dishes were 'fence' (Irish stew) and 'pterodactyl', a kind of beef hot-pot; but everything Mollie cooked tasted like a banquet.

In the mid-Fifties Mollie's brother, Rupert, came to live with us. Another breadwinner in the house helped considerably and the chil-dren were devoted to him. During his stay we again became road users in the shape of a succession of extraordinary cars and vans. One of these, which had been presented to me by a retiring master at All Hallows, had a garden on the running board and would only turn in one direction, to the left; any attempt to turn right immediately applied the brakes. A visit to Bath in this car was an adventure which I do not wish to repeat.

After our visit to Ireland I decided that we could not afford seaside holidays, but we often went for day trips to the sea. The most frequent outing was to Beer in South Devon. We would start early in whatever derelict car was running at the time and arrive about midday. Then we would call at a cottage where, by previous arrangement, crabs had been cooked for us. These we would take down to our special cave on the beach and devour, cracking the claws with stones. Nets were next produced and some went prawning while others went out mackerel fishing or swimming. More than once we had driven half way home before discovering that towels and bathing dresses had been left behind.

Another regular outing was the visit to the dentist in Bath. Mollie never came with us; she always said that she would rather have a baby than go to the dentist. Rupert and Cicely never had to have any treatment, but Rachel was always in trouble; she used to fight the dentist both physically and verbally, while he kept shouting 'Open your mouth – this minute'. Afterwards we would drive out into the country to eat a picnic lunch, which always contained prawns; then back into Bath to the cinema. This helped to atone for the horrors of the dentist. In due course the children's teeth gave less trouble because Mollie began to make bread. It benefited not only us but many who came to buy it. In fact before we left Chilcompton we had an extensive bread round, which introduced us to many new friends and helped the finances.

As far back as 1948 my father had been appointed Archdeacon of Ludlow. He had been twenty years at Hammersmith and was quite ready to leave, especially as his appointment enabled him to live at Quatford. I attended his installation at Hereford Cathedral and admired his gaitered calves. The next six years at Quatford made serious inroads into his finances: the estate produced an exiguous income and the salary of an archdeacon was little more than £300 per annum. My parents decided to pay off their mortgage by selling the castle and taking over a parish, which was to be Stanton Lacy, near Ludlow. It was heart-rending to see the castle go; it had been in our family since it was built in 1830 and was full of memories for me. Stanton Lacy had a beautiful Saxon church and large vicarage. There relays of my children would be invited to stay with their grandparents and I usually took them. Mother and Father had by now recovered from the blow which I had dealt them by becoming a Catholic. I think my appointment to Downside had done much to effect this recovery. Sometimes I stayed on for a few days, but I usually left a few children at Stanton Lacy and returned home. Maurice, now gaining a reputation as a singer, had married in 1948 and his daughter, Jessica, used to stay with them.

In 1957 Joe was born. Coming on a day when he was not expected, I had gone to school. As Mollie's pains suddenly began, she noticed that the goat had tangled itself in its chain; she untied the goat then telephoned Nurse Bird, the midwife, and the school. In a few minutes we arrived; the goat was peacefully grazing and Joe was born upstairs that evening, while I was frying fish and chips for the children's supper.

By 1960 we were beginning to think of schools for the children. They had done well under Mona, but the older ones needed more advanced education and Mona was thinking of new pastures; she obtained a post at St Richard's, Little Malvern. John was no problem, since he was old enough to go to Downside as a day boy. David and Tony were very musical and, although it meant sending them away, we decided that they would benefit from a choir school education. They were accepted by Westminster Cathedral with a generous grant from St Hugh's Society, which covered their fees. They were followed in due course by Rupert and Joe. Since they had to sing on Sundays, as well as weekdays, there was no chance of weekends at home. Instead the first Wednesday of each month was designated as a holiday, a plan originally made for London boys, and difficult for us to accommodate. We had them home for the short time, however, even though the joys of homecoming were swiftly drowned by the miseries of separation. Going back to school after the holidays was heart rending. David was old enough to bottle up his tears, but Tony began to cry two days before he went back. I asked them both many years later whether they had thought boarding worthwhile. They both answered that they would not have missed the choir for the world.

Mary and Gwen, the two elder girls, went to St Antony's, Leweston; again we were offered such generous terms that we could hardly have refused, even if we had wished to. I took Mary to school in May 1960. Leaving her in the care of Mother Eleanor, the Headmistress, I could hardly steer down the drive, my eyes were so misted with tears. Gwen followed the next term, but did not stay out her full time; either the school did not suit her, or she did not suit the school; she transferred after three years to the convent at Shepton Mallet, where the academic requirements were less arduous. Many of our family have been late developers: at the age of forty-five, Gwen was to gain an MA degree in English.

Meanwhile the family was increased by four. Jeremy, born in 1958, had a bad start. Unfortunately, when he was about one year old and still crawling about on the floor, he crawled underneath the car, while I was in the house. Not knowing this, I started to move off to school, felt the back of the car lift up and rushed round to see what had happened; the back wheel had run over Jeremy. He was not crying – a bad sign – so I picked him up and carried him over to the doctor opposite. I had to take him to hospital in Bath, where they found that he had a fractured femur. They put weights on his legs. He took all this very well and a few days later was throwing the weights all over the ward and jerking his cot wherever he fancied. After his return home, a month later, he took a long time to fit into the family and spent much of the day crying. He did, in fact, present us with a problem all through his young life and it was not until many years later, when he discovered that a nursing career was what he really wanted, that he settled down to a normal, happy life. Stella, born shortly after Christmas 1959, had no such problems. Blessed with a sunny disposition and considerable physical beauty, she sailed happily through her childhood, as did her younger sister, Helen, born in April 1961. Helen suffered badly from eczema and asthma, both family weaknesses, but I do not remember her complaining. Daniel was born during the bitter cold of January 1963 on New Year's Day. Mollie had to be driven by ambulance into Bath to reach St Martin's Hospital during New Year's Eve celebrations. Daniel, unlike our usual models, had dark hair and a swarthy complexion. The mother in the bed next to Mollie was a Mrs Cohen, and but for the fact that Daniel's long nose and love of wine and fish betray his Bevan ancestry, one might have been pardoned for wondering whether the medical staff in its midnight revels had not made a mistake; in later life he was the first boy to earn a large salary. As a baby he was quiet and amenable.

As might have been expected, money was through these years an ever-increasing worry. I had enough to do at Downside, but had to go on teaching at All Hallows, taking on extra work with private pupils and at Shepton Mallet Convent. At Downside I taught all GCE music at both levels, organ and elementary trumpet and trombone; in addition I was responsible for the organisation of the department and the conducting of concerts. Even with all this, however, the budget did not balance. One morning one of my bank managers (I used two banks) telephoned to say that I had to pay £10 into my account before the close of business that day. In fact this, as I discovered later, was the bank's fault, as it had deducted from my account a post-dated cheque. Where was I to find £10? I remembered that a friend of mine, Fr. Bruno Scott-James had frequently told me that the greatest compliment he could be paid was to be asked to lend money. I decided to pay him this compliment and asked if I could come over and see him. I duly arrived and as the bottle of Chambertin, which we were discussing, began to draw to an end, I tried to pluck up my courage to ask the question. Just as I was about to speak the telephone rang; it was Mollie, who asked to speak to me; 'Don't ask for anything; I've sold the pig'. I returned to my seat and helped to finish the wine.

Amidst these troubles came one worse still. Downside Lodge had been in a bad state of repair from the beginning. For ten years since then it had resounded to the patter of tiny feet and the batter of larger ones; it was showing signs of extreme wear. The first thing we noticed was a sudden crunch in the middle of Sunday lunch, when the leg of the bed in the room above came through the kitchen ceiling. The Bursar was growing tired of sending builders and carpenters over to us, so he ordered an expensive architect to come out from Bath and advise him. In due course I was told that it would cost £10,000 to repair the house. Had the Bursar known, he could have recovered his outlay, because property rose in value considerably between 1964 and 1974; but he was not to know that. I received a letter giving me a year's notice to quit. This was a blow indeed; I had no capital and had accepted the Downside post expressly on terms which included a house. The Bursar, Fr. Vincent Kavanagh, was not very sympathetic and merely hinted that if I preferred, I could leave.

By this time Fr. Wilfrid had retired from the Head Mastership and his successor, Dom Aehed Watkin, whom I both liked and admired, did not feel it appropriate to intervene in this matter. It was our bread round which solved the money problem. One of our customers was John Eke, who worked for an insurance firm in Bristol and was shortly to form his own in Midsomer Norton. He suddenly came forward with an offer from Westminster Cathedral of a 100% mortgage to enable us to buy a house. I was never more surprised in my life; no one would tell me who had made this magnificent offer and I never discovered. If he is reading this book, I would like him to know how he changed all our lives for the better and how grateful the whole family is. Now we could begin house hunting.

Every afternoon we could spare at weekends we drove out in the car, looking at houses within reach of Downside. None of them seemed suitable: they were either too derelict, too expensive or were standing in the middle of a field of mud with cows grazing right up to the walls. One day we visited some properties the other side of Wells; on the way home we passed through Croscombe and noticed a farmhouse raised slightly above the road in the centre of the village; there was a large 'For Sale' notice on the gable. 'That's our house' cried Mollie and we drove up the hill.

The sole occupant was Elizabeth Barrand, who farmed the land single handed. She was the daughter of an eye specialist in Bristol, but she had opted out of town life and 'gone native'. After various negotiations we bought the property, comprising a five-bedroomed house, copious outhouses and a two-acre field, for £4,500. It was the best thing we ever did and changed our fortunes when we grew old. We arranged

to move in October 1965 and were assisted in our move by a host of
friends, who turned up in their cars to transport the more fragile items
of furniture. It was very touching that they should have helped in that
way. After the move we gave them a very alcoholic party.

# CHAPTER XIII

❧

# *Downside Abbey (2)*

John Buckley left Downside in 1959 for Trinidad, where he was to take up a Director of Music's post at a Benedictine school. Arriving there he found that his salary classed him as a 'poor white'; he told me that he and the art master had to walk to school, while the cars of the prosperous natives spattered them with mud. He stayed only a year but then managed to secure the music directorship at Worth. I think he would have been happier if he had stayed on at Downside. I certainly would. His place was taken by Dennis Hartley as Bandmaster and Peter Matthews who outstayed me as piano teacher.

The gym was burnt down in 1956. It had been a ramshackle, wooden building. The dirt of ages seemed to be ingrained in the fabric: I remember a performance by a troupe of Spanish dancers on the stage at one end of the hall. It was almost impossible to distinguish between *fandango* and *bolero*, so thick was the cloud of dust which rose from the floor with each movement. At the end the Spanish performers were furious to find their long dresses turned black.

I arrived at school one autumn morning to find the two dingy music rooms about to be consumed by an approaching conflagration: willing hands were ready to sort out the instruments while there was still time. It was unfortunately impossible to throw the grand piano out of the window; it would have been worth saving; the wind instruments were carefully sorted and those in bad need of repair were left behind. We needed new school violins, so we did not bother to rescue the old ones. No one ever discovered the cause of the fire: some said it was the electricity, others the Head Master.

We took temporary refuge in the Armoury until three Nissen huts were erected to accommodate string and wind players; they were by no means sound-proof and many a violinist had to contend with a chorus of trombones a few yards away. It seemed, however, that as the facilities deteriorated, the enthusiasm of the boys increased. Those were days when every boy above the fifth form had his own private time-table in which hours of class work would be interspersed with periods of private study, into which music could easily be fitted. Apart from university awards, the rat race for examination success had not yet reached Downside and some boys found it possible, although not recommended, to spend whole days in the music huts. In 1957 we carried off seven first prizes out of seven entries at the Mid-Somerset Festival.

In 1960, I negotiated with Mother Eleanor, headmistress of St Antony's Girls' School, Leweston, to join our choral societies together, so that we could tackle more ambitious works. By 1961 a new theatre had been built and we were able to perform Bach's St Matthew Passion there in the spring. I believe that I was the first to introduce girls into a performance at Downside. It was a sign of the growing disintegration of the old fashioned Public School with its closed society. Abbot Butler, who disliked music, was persuaded by one of the monks to attend the performance. He lasted until St Peter's denial, perhaps the most movingly dramatic part of the whole work; while St Peter wept bitterly, the Abbot rose from his tip-up seat and with a clatter stumped out of the hall.

Several well-known singers cut their teeth on our performances; Janet Baker sang at our Messiah and Christmas Oratorio, John Carol Case at the Mozart Coronation Mass, John Shirley-Quirk at the Mozart Requiem which we sang also in Westminster Cathedral Hall. Most of these singers were at a very early stage in their careers. It was a wonderful experience for the boys and girls to be making music with artists of such calibre.

Three times a term we had a joint rehearsal at Leweston. On the first occasion we arrived to find the whole community of nuns, headed by Reverend Mother, lined up on the steps to meet us; every boy had to pass along the line shaking hands. After a few terms the nuns grew more used to us and there was less formality. They used to give us a wonderful tea at the end. On one occasion Reverend Mother, a Belgian, took me aside and gave me a long talk about our boys taking girls round the school grounds, in case they should 'do ze bad sings'. In fact the only 'bad sings' they did, as far as I know, were to smoke and drop their cigarette ends into the lavatory. Unfortunately Dom Gregory Murray, who had come as accompanist, saw these; instead of telling me, he saw fit to inform the Head Master, thereby causing a great deal of trouble. A typewritten envelope was on the Common Room table for me next morning: not the sack, but a withdrawal of his permission to perform the St Matthew Passion. I was dumbfounded; there were only four weeks to go before the performance; the soloists and orchestra were booked and another school was involved. For about two weeks Dom Theodore James, an influential housemaster – if anyone could be called influential with Dom Wilfrid – pleaded my case but with no effect. I finally made up my mind to approach the Head Master myself and was ready with my resignation if he refused me. It was typical of his quixotic character that my reception was the opposite of what I expected. 'Come in, come in, my dear, what is the problem?' He smiled blandly. When I told him with some asperity, he answered: 'Why, of course you must perform the St Matthew Passion; we can't let down all those people, can we?'

We usually practised at Leweston. Downside was less easy to manage, especially catering for so many visitors. On one occasion my choral society ate not only their own tea but another, provided for the chess club. I received a four-page letter from the monk in charge and had to write a tricky apology. At Leweston there were no such problems. At first I was dismayed to have my rehearsals monitored by Eileen Likeman, the Director of Music, and Joyce Sutton, the choir mistress. I suppose they thought that I was either inefficient or likely to flirt with the girls. This did not last, however, and before long I won the privilege of being asked by them for advice. The girls were always so beautifully trained both by Joyce and her successor, Jane Stein, that they constituted the main attraction of our long series of concerts from 1961 to 1984.

Through all this period the Headmistress, Mother Eleanor, was a rock of support and common sense. A strong personality, she knew her girls thoroughly – even what was going on in their minds. All of my six daughters were educated by her and acknowledge the influence she brought to bear.

After each Leweston rehearsal the Downside contingent stopped for supper at a public house *en route*: the Mildmay Arms at Queen Camel, the Sherston Hotel, Wells, the Strode Arms at Cranmore or the Bull Terrier at Croscombe. In the days when outings were rare except for matches, and certainly did not involve the society of girls, these rehearsals did much to increase the contentment and stability of the boys in their otherwise cloistered life.

Entertainment of visitors at Downside was never in those days an easy matter: on one occasion I had invited Germani, the celebrated Italian organist, to give a recital in the Abbey church. I sent a taxi to meet him at Bath station with 'Downside School' clearly printed on the windscreen. There was, however, at Bath a large notice displayed in the station, pointing to DOWN SIDE, meaning the opposite platform. Germani waited there where the taxi driver could not find him. Finally he took a bus to Stratton and I found him waiting outside the Head Master's study, sitting on a bench used by those waiting to be caned. He had been there an hour. I rescued him and took him home for a belated meal.

During the late Fifties a new figure arrived on the music staff in the person of Leslie Calvert. He was a Mus.B. of Cambridge, ex-organist of Oswestry Parish church and a competent pianist. I needed someone like that to help with piano and some of the paperwork. Things, however, did not turn out well. He was a sad, lonely person, the son of a forceful mother, with a strangely warped attitude towards his fellow creatures. He was wildly enthusiastic about his friends but almost sadistic towards those he considered his enemies. At first I belonged to the first category, but was always on guard lest I should descend without warning into the second. His pupils were not excluded from this treatment.

In one direction, however, Calvy, as he was called, behaved admirably. He was extremely fond of small children and would spend hours with mine, visiting our house every day, lighting bonfires and organising games for them. We were sorry to lose him when he discovered a vocation to the monastic life and entered the noviciate at Worth. His residence there lasted precisely forty-eight hours, after which he took refuge in the bar of a local hotel. After a year or two in various posts, he returned to Downside, but not for long. He soon turned against Mollie and me and began to speak against me to the boys in the school. He left and I never saw him again until the 1980s. Having forgotten his previous complaints, he again became a regular visitor, but was still lonely and unhappy until he died. The only people at his funeral, beside myself, were Dom Gervase from Downside and his executor, a solicitor-cousin. I always liked Calvy; he had a wonderful sense of humour.

Another eccentric musician who joined us was Cedric Beadle, a cellist who also taught at Bryanston. He was always comparing Downside to Bryanston, to our disadvantage, of course. He was an excellent teacher but his appearance and manner made him a figure of fun to some of the boys. On one occasion, while he was standing outside one of the Houses, some rude boys began to shout derisively at him. Suddenly a car appeared driving slowly down from the monastery; it contained the Abbot, Dom John Roberts. Cedric held up his hand, stopped the car and addressed the Abbot: 'See those boys up there? You ought to go and stop them.' When Dom John suggested that this lay more in the Head Master's province, Cedric shouted: 'Call yourself an Abbot? They wouldn't be allowed to do that at Bryanston.'

No picture of Downside in the Sixties would be complete without mention of the annual visit of Surgeon-Commander Sinclair-Loutit: this took place at the end of the summer term. Every morning he would sit in his ancient car with his ferocious dog, waiting for boys, or occasionally masters, to go up and talk to him. Masters were acknowledged only if the dog approved, which was seldom, but I was one of the lucky ones. The boys would be taken for drives, in which the Commander kept to the middle of the road, cursing loudly and obscenely anyone who tried to pass him. I was invited to his lodgings to imbibe quantities of orange gin, a sickly but extremely potent drink. In fact I think I spent the examination weeks in a permanent haze of alcohol.

Loutit had been at Downside in the 1890s and sang in the choir under Sir Richard Terry, who worked there before his appointment to Westminster Cathedral. The boys, I was told, hated Palestrina. The Commander used often to attend our rehearsals at Leweston, after which he passed round the bottle freely at the pub. He even entertained the Choral Society at the Crown Hotel in Wells. Like so many of his type, he had violent dislikes, one of which was Bill Smethurst, the violin teacher. One evening he summoned the waiter and shouted: 'Wine for everybody – except for that little fellow with red hair, sitting at the far end.' It was a miracle that no boys were killed on his motor expeditions and that I did not become an alcoholic.

We managed a few musical distinctions during the Sixties and early Seventies: my son David won a music scholarship to Queen's, Oxford; Tony an exhibition to St John's, Cambridge; Bernard Trafford an organ scholarship to St Edmund Hall, Oxford, and Philip Fowke a piano scholarship to the Royal Academy of Music. Philip became a professional concert pianist and figured in several promenade concerts. None of these musicians, alas, has ever become rich. Professional music is a passport to poverty. My father always said 'music is a splendid companion but a difficult mistress.' How right he was.

When I came to Downside, I had no musical qualification. I therefore decided to remedy this and prepare for the Mus.B. degree at Trinity College, Dublin. Oxford would not have been possible because the B.Mus. there is a second degree and I did not read music for my first. With much of the work I was already familiar; I travelled to Ireland in 1959 for Part I, which caused me no trouble academically. I did however have an embarrassing experience in the hotel. The day before the examination was a Sunday; after a copious lunch of mutton chops and cabbage, I retired to the lounge for some last minute revision. I had not been sitting there for fifteen minutes before an enormous crowd of drunken Irishmen invaded the room: a large man staggered up and swayed in front of me: 'Ireland's greatest poet' whispered a voice in my ear; but Ireland's greatest poet did not recite, he waved a Guinness bottle at me and shouted 'Say something.' I was tongue-tied 'Say something, or I will brain you with this bottle', he continued. I murmured some platitude and he turned his attention elsewhere. Plainly there would be no revision here, so I walked down the road to Molesworth Street, the only time that name has been a comfort to me. I entered Buswell's Hotel and was immediately in my element: gaitered legs betokened the presence of dignitaries of the Church of Ireland, in which nearly every cleric is a Dean or Archdeacon. After tea and crumpets I settled down to my revision undisturbed.

Pressure of school work delayed Part II for four years, during which I had to write a string quartet. The final examination was more searching and I had to have tuition from Kenneth Mobbs at Bristol University. For the result I was not kept long in suspense; it was posted up within three hours of the last paper; I had passed. I took ship for home feeling elated and decided to celebrate with dinner and a bottle of wine in the restaurant. I noticed that the waiter handed the food to me with a lugubrious air of disapproval, so I asked him why he was so gloomy: 'Didn't you know, sir, President Kennedy was assassinated this after-noon?' I then saw that the whole ship seemed to be in mourning and that there was no one else in the restaurant. I said a *De Profundis* for the President and finished the wine, my chief thought being that I was now a Bachelor of Music.

When I first joined the staff at Downside in 1953 the boys spent a good deal of their time in church. Daily Mass was said not only at the High Altar but in all the side-chapels from which the tinkling of sanctus bells could be heard from 7.30 am to 9 am each morning. I was from the time of my first visit intensely moved by this. There was also Bene-diction during the week; on Sunday morning there were Terce and Solemn High Mass with the whole monastic community; in the even-ing, Sung Vespers. The boys therefore played a considerable part in the life of the monastery. The school choir, in deference to prevailing fashion, had been disbanded in 1942 and their singing replaced by congregational plainsong. A few hymns were sung from a home-made book, the *Cantionale*. It had been compiled by Dom Cuthbert McCann, but there was difficulty in finding the hymns, as there was no index. If my mother had been a monk, she would not have found that a problem.

Vatican II heralded a drastic reduction in religious observance, so that by 1969 everything had disappeared except the School Mass on

*Mollie at Borth (1961)*

*Monsignor Tony and Bishop David Bevan (1963)*

*RHB. Downside Lodge (1965)*

*Downside Lodge being demolished (1965).*

*Mollie at Gwen's wedding (1970)*

*The family in 1967. Back row: Cicely, David, Mary, Gwen, RHB, Mollie, John, Rachel. Front row: Tony, Jeremy, Rupert, Joe, Stella, Helen. In front: Daniel (Ben not yet born)*

*All Hallows choir (1985)*

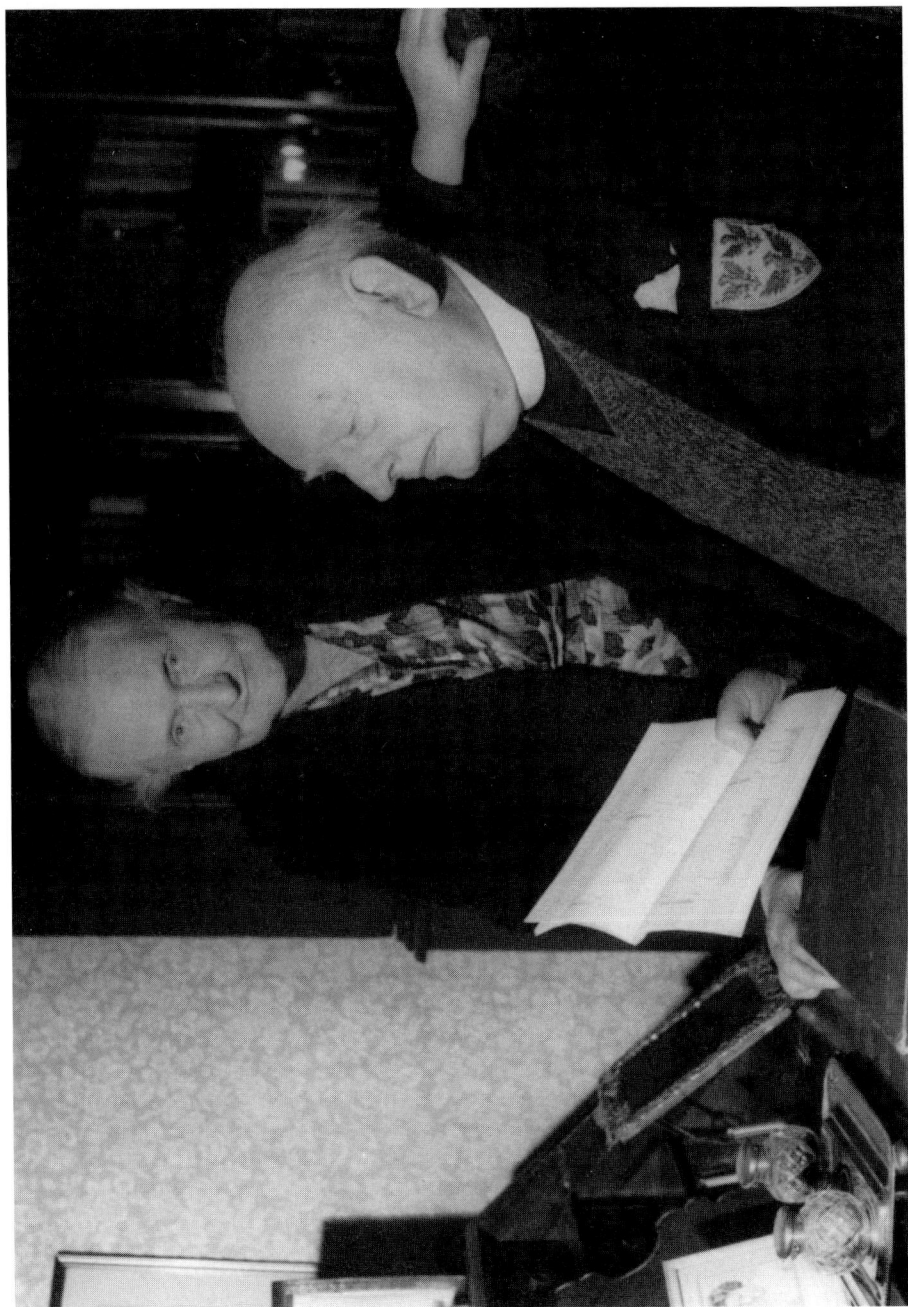

*Father and Mother, golden wedding (1967)*

*Most of the family at Tony's wedding (1987)*

*Concert at Edington Priory (1991)*

Sunday, Vespers, which ceased after a year, and Benediction, which continued for about a further fourteen years.

The change to English caused a reaction against plainsong and led to a call for a more varied selection of hymns. Dom Gregory provided 'A Downside Mass', which was of higher quality than his more popular 'Peoples' Mass', but I thought it an uninspired composition. I composed another and for a few years we performed the two Masses alternately, until a new translation arrived in 1972. Dom Gregory rewrote his Mass, but I consigned mine to the bonfire. I also produced a new *Cantionale*, which is still in use.

In 1968 the School Mass had migrated to the theatre, while the Abbey church was being reconstructed for the new site. Dom Edward Crouzet at this time formed a choir of tenors and basses. Downside had been designated as a place of 'liturgical experiment' of which the resurgence of the choir was one of the happier results.

When the church was brought back into use in 1969, Dom Aelred Watkin asked me to take over the church music of the School. This was the post I had originally accepted in 1953, but had not been allowed to fill. I had always wished for it and, indeed, felt more competent to tackle this work than any other musical activity. I thought it would put me into closer touch with the School as a whole, and so it proved.

At first I played the organ and directed the choir from the console. The Abbey organ is a famous instrument, built in 1931 by John Compton and a prototype of the organ in Broadcasting House. It has a fine tone, especially in the softer registers and is ideal for plainsong accompaniment. It has, however, a vast number of 'gadgets' which are liable to go wrong. Some of the pistons are so sensitive that a portly organist can easily, with a waistcoat button, switch in a split second from sweet and tender flutes to roaring tubas and bombards. After about two years I secured the services of Peter Matthews as organist, while I attended to the choir.

I was able to train the Schola in a repertory of anthems, leading eventually to polyphonic settings of parts of the Mass. It was good to have a small number of enthusiastic singers at a time when congregational singing – and, it seemed, religion itself – was at a low ebb. All the congregation seemed prepared to sing was the last verse of the final hymn. There was a demand for guitars, which I steadfastly resisted. Of all instruments the guitar is for accompanying massed voices the worst. One Sunday a group of guitarists from the school was, unknown to me, smuggled into the front pew. At the Offertory they struck up; the sound was so feeble and amateurish that everybody laughed.

*Tantum religio potuit suadere malorum*

They never tried again.

Preserving a good standard of music in the modern Church is a difficult task. The traditional idea that the function of church music is to lift the heart and soul to God is now unfashionable, although I believe it to be true. Nowadays stress is put on 'participation', which is construed as joining vocally in hymns and in the singing of the Mass. It would help the cause of true worship if we thought at Mass more about what was happening and less about the sound of our own voices. Congregational singing of English hymns was imported into this country from Geneva during the reign of Elizabeth I; it embodies a Protestant attitude to worship and is greatly overdone in Catholic churches today. 'Be still and know that I am God', says the psalm. What better than to meditate on that while the music of Palestrina and Victoria soars to the roof with the incense rising with it?

One can become wearied by the continued and often uncharitable criticisms made by traditional Catholics of the new Mass. These would have been avoided if the old Roman Mass, nowadays mis-named 'Tridentine', had been allowed to survive in parallel with the new. It contains sound doctrine and can be traced back to the earliest centuries of European civilisation. The present Pope is known to desire it to be available to all, but some fault in the chain of authority has prevented this.

There were important developments during the mid-1970s, the chief being the opening of Plunkett House, our own prep school, in 1975. This entailed more work for the music staff, but we managed, with difficulty, to absorb the newcomers without increasing the number of teachers. The music department had by now moved to new premises in the village. One advantage was that we could now produce a proper choir with trebles in the Abbey church, whereas previously we had only altos, tenors and basses, with whom we had already broadcast Mass on television and sound radio. My choral ambitions, however, did not meet with ready acceptance; after two terms, when the trebles were ready, they were restricted to fortnightly sung masses. As the standard gradually rose it became necessary to station the singers in two groups facing each other across the nave. Immediately the old anti-music syndrome reappeared; one housemaster objected because the choir interfered with his boys' view of the altar; another wanted the choristers relegated to a side chapel where they could neither see nor be heard. I was forced to crowd them all on to one side. It was galling to observe that, when I gave up the post of choir master, the monk who succeeded me had no difficulty in placing his choir on two sides. In addition to these indignities I was for a time forced to obey the orders of a monk who had been appointed 'Precentor'. He knew little about church music and insisted that we performed 'trendy' music of little or no artistic value. In spite of all this, however, I enjoyed my fifteen years in charge of the Schola. We performed much good and interesting music and I think can claim to have given some boys an abiding interest. The summit of our annual efforts was the carol service in which the choir of Wells Cathedral took part. This originated in the time before we had our own trebles, but continued afterwards as an ecumenical gesture and not, as some would have it, because we could not manage on our own. One other occasion I remember was the visit of the Apostolic Delegate, for which I composed an *Ecce Sacerdos Magnus*. The choir provided some of the best singing I ever heard them produce – and we heard the worst sermon.

In 1983 I was suddenly informed that my services in the Abbey Church would not be required after July. This was because a monk had recently emerged from the Community who was a qualified musician and able to take over. It was thought more appropriate that a monk should hold the post. It was a tremendous wrench for me, especially as the Schola had been invited to sing in Wells Cathedral during the following autumn. No one, however, is indispensable, and I had only one more year to run as Director of Music at the school. Apart from my being sixty-six, my presence at home was beginning to be necessary, since Mollie's health was declining. I therefore retired in 1984 after thirty-one years.

I am eternally grateful to Downside, chiefly for educating my eight sons, but also for the friendly relations which I enjoyed with so many of the Community. Notable among these was Dom Cuthbert McCann; he took part in every performance which I organised and loyally supported me over the years. During every holiday time we used to go out together on an expedition in the car and we explored large tracts of Somerset, Dorset and Wiltshire in this way. On one visit to Lulworth Cove, we walked past a pond full of quite ordinary ducks. Fr. Cuthbert stopped and stared at them, amazed: 'Look! Exotic birds!' he cried. He had a very simple and uncomplicated mind and was liable to take seriously what was said as a figure of speech. While we were discussing the installation of the Prince of Wales at Caernarvon Castle, I remarked that the singing did not exactly raise the roof; he replied 'Oh, but there wasn't a roof.' We continued our expeditions together until a week before he died. I miss him greatly.

# CHAPTER XIV

❧

# *All Hallows*

Throughout these years I continued my ministrations at All Hallows. The recorder classes had disappeared and I confined myself to choir practices and piano lessons during the afternoons. In the early Sixties Mr Dix moved out of the school and appointed a deputy to look after its affairs, while he and Mrs Dix went to live at Charlton House, just outside Shepton Mallet. They had a dozen boys boarding there at increased fees enjoying, supposedly, home comforts. I was invited to dine there one night; the beverage traditionally offered was Emu Burgundy; Dix duly uncorked the bottle and began to pour; 'Good heavens!' he exclaimed, 'it's red'. In 1972 he retired to Wells, travelling by taxi to All Hallows several times a week to teach Latin. The school became a charitable trust with a governing body and a new, salaried headmaster was appointed.

It has generally been my lot to serve under unmusical headmasters or abbots. This had advantages, as they left me to get on without interference. The new headmaster of All Hallows was not one of these; he knew a little about music, enough to criticise the choir and even deprive them of their annual treat if he thought they had not given their best. I was not consulted. On the other hand, he allowed me extra practice time whenever I needed it, for which the boys' academic work must have suffered. Morale in the school was not very high, since the headmaster was greatly addicted to the cane; the standard of teaching declined, being mainly in the hands of ex-army officers, few of whom were vocational schoolmasters. One mathematics teacher was extremely unpopular, especially with two boys, whose parents removed them from the school. Next term at their new school they sat down for a mathematics class and beheld the same teacher at his desk; he had left All Hallows at the same time.

Towards the end of the Sixties the numbers at All Hallows began to decline. There was no parallel loss in other schools and it became clear that there had to be a change. I remember one dreadful scene when someone dropped some wire into the swimming pool. The whole school was paraded and the culprit ordered to confess. No confession was forthcoming and the boys were kept standing for three hours. When they finally had their lunch at three o'clock, it was cold. I was so incensed about this that I refused to teach and drove off to Downside and later spoke to Abbot Passmore, who was chairman of the governors. When the chaplain (the same who had expressed his dislike of me when I first came to Downside) heard of it, he exclaimed 'Why did Bevan make such a fool of himself? He could have had *his* lunch!' Eventually the headmaster left and things began to improve; in fact it could be said that the Seventies and Eighties were the golden age of All Hallows.

Paul Ketterer, the next headmaster, had a flair for organisation. This played an important part in generating a happy atmosphere among the pupils: nothing makes children happier than being part of a well regulated society; the first thing which still strikes the visitors to All Hallows is the happiness and good manners of the pupils. The prevailing euphoria did not, on the whole, animate the staff; good relationships with his colleagues was not Paul's strong point and he was plagued with staff troubles for most of his tenure of office. He set out at once to increase the number of pupils by admitting girls. All Hallows was one of the first independent schools to become co-educational with regard both to boarders and day pupils. The presence of girls revolutionised the character of the school: the boys became more civilised and had to work harder to keep up with the girls, who at that age are more mature.

I had not taught girls since Newtown days and found the change refreshing. An increasing number joined the Chapel Choir, but I was always careful to keep the number of boys and girls roughly equal, to avoid the boys being taken over. The girls, however, were always great supporters of the choir.

Mallowan's successor as French master had been Martin Blake, with whom I have kept up a continuous friendship even after he departed to be head of French at Worth. He was an Oxford graduate at a time when such birds were rare in prep schools. Nowadays there are far more universities and nearly all the teachers are both graduates and qualified teachers. Dix would never employ anyone possessing a teacher's certificate, nor would he admit coloured boys into the school.

The school had changed very much since Francis Dix's time and was now run on highly professional lines. Unfortunately, but, I suppose, unavoidably, the number of non-Catholic pupils increased until they greatly outweighed the Catholic population. This was also the case with the staff. A kind of religious syncretism arose in which the distinction between Catholics and Protestants became progressively more vague. Most of the staff, a few stalwarts excepted, believed that one religion was as good as another and that the distinction between Catholic and Protestant beliefs was a creation of old-fashioned modes of thought which had no place in the brave new world. This is a doctrine widely accepted even outside All Hallows, but it is wildly misleading. Catholics believe in a Church, to which was given by Jesus Christ a mission to teach all nations, interpreting to them the revelations given to it by Him. We accept our beliefs on the authority of that Church, or the Magisterium, as it is called. Protestants exercise their private judgement on all things: doctrines such as the Trinity or the Real Presence in the Eucharist are all placed at the bar of private judgement, whereas the human mind is incapable of discovering unaided the truth of these mysteries; they are acceptable only as part of a supernatural revelation. The craze for ecumenism has obliterated this basic truth, and because of this religion generally has been weakened.

Even in Catholic schools there has been a general decline in the quality of religious teaching. At Downside in the Seventies, I tried, with Fr. Cuthbert's help, to restore the Corpus Christi procession. The result was disastrous: the boys made fun of it and plainly had never been taught what it was all about. Doubtless that has now been remedied, but if that can happen in a Catholic school, what is the case with a school which is less than one half Catholic?

When I eventually retired from Downside in 1984 I visualised the days stretching ahead and crying to be filled with something for me to do. It did not turn out like that. I still had my All Hallows work at which Paul Ketterer said that I could stay as long as I liked. I was no longer restricted to afternoon work, so that it became possible to spread my classes and increase their number. I was especially pleased to be able to give more time to the choir; the standard of its singing rose considerably during the next ten years and was enhanced both by the building of a new chapel with an organ and by the advent of Rachel as singing teacher; she helped enormously with voice production. We were thus able to make a cassette in 1985 and sing Mass at Brompton Oratory, Westminster Cathedral and the Oratory at Oxford. We also gave a half-hour recital at Wells Cathedral and Prior Park.

I enjoyed my last ten years at All Hallows almost more than any other period of my teaching life. It was a bitter blow when in 1994 I was told that the direction of the Chapel Choir was to be given to another and that my services would be required no longer. My dismissal was so sudden that some must have thought I had committed some crime; this, however, was not the case. The ways of Providence are inscrutable.

# CHAPTER XV

❧

# *Family Life*

Our move to Croscombe in 1965 took us away from the rapidly spreading suburbia of Radstock and Midsomer Norton into the open countryside of real Somerset. The village occupies two sides of a narrow valley between Shepton Mallet and Wells on what is called the River Sheppey; its real name is Doulting Water, for it rises at St Aldhelm's Well in Doulting. Croscombe is full of old stone-built cottages, of which our new house, Parsonage Farm, comprised three. They were originally farm labourers' cottages next to the old parsonage, but had been joined into one house many years earlier. We had five outhouses and a large modern barn which had been a milking shed before we arrived. Behind the house was a two-acre field, facing north up the hillside. We should have plenty of room for animals. Although we had kept a cow at Downside Lodge (we rented fields from other residents) we decided against it at Croscombe, since it entailed so much work; we eventually decided on sheep, two goats, geese, pigs and hens.

Six months after we left Downside Lodge a crane with an iron ball arrived. The seventeenth century house was reduced to rubble within three days; the site was cleared and sold to developers. A crop of bungaloid growths has replaced the house we loved.

The mortgage interest I had to pay amounted to more than the rent I had paid for Downside Lodge, so that another period of poverty ensued. The coal merchant grew agitated and there were bills everywhere. A gold filling fell out of one of my teeth and I thought I would turn it into cash. Alas, the total sum offered to me for it in Bath was 4/6d (22p)! In all my financial crises I have been providentially delivered from disaster: this time it was Uncle Hughe, who sent me, completely by surprise, a cheque for £500. He had received it in return for the film rights of Aunt Flo's book *Misunderstood*. He had by now retired to

Barham, near Canterbury, was well provided for and thought that I might find a use for it; how right he was!

Many friends have asked me how we managed to look after such a large family. The most difficult time was in the early Sixties, before the older ones began to leave home. During school holidays, after Daniel was born, we had all thirteen children in the house, aged between one and sixteen. The older children were able to help and at one time I pinned up duty rosters, a most unpopular move. It was more satisfactory in the end to leave them to sort out the jobs by themselves. There were three girls able to put the little ones to bed; at least two could cook and many more could wash up and dry. When I was not out at school, I used to change nappies, cook a meal or put children to bed. The boys also learnt to cook and most of them are highly proficient.

Before we left Downside Lodge the daily routine was something like this: after getting up at about 7.30, either Mollie or I, or both of us, would drive down to milk the cow, taking with us Tony and Rupert (aged 8 and 6). Others, such as John and Mary, could also milk if necessary. The girls would get the others up and prepare breakfast, while John fed the hens and pigs. After breakfast I would drive Rachel, Cicely, Rupert, Joe and Jeremy either to Shepton Convent or to the bus stop before going on myself to Downside for the morning's work. Mollie would spend the morning either washing (we had a machine by now), making bread or scrubbing the kitchen floor. She loved scrubbing and often said that she would like to earn some money by scrubbing other people's floors. We had someone in to help with the housework, since she could not have managed it all on her own.

I always came home for lunch; in fact I always made a point of coming home whenever I could, as it was good for morale, both mine and the family's. There are few things which cause more unhappiness to a wife than her husband's absence all and every day. After lunch on some days I went off for my stint at All Hallows or Shepton Convent. Otherwise I stayed at home and read to Mollie for about two hours, returning to Downside for three more classes, finishing at seven. On some days I had to stay on for Choral Society or some other activity after the boys' supper. Failing that I went home to help with the children's supper and bedtime, which included prayers and a story. I was not very good at making up stories, since I do not possess that kind of imagination. Mollie, on the other hand, used to make up the most splendid children's stories I have ever heard. She had her audience crying with laughter; I wish she had written them down. We never had a television set, thank goodness.

In 1965, a few months before we moved house, we suffered the tragedy of a stillborn child. Bridget was a little girl with beautiful golden hair; she had died through strangulation by the cord; the midwife (not Nurse Bird, but her successor) had left the resuscitator at her house and I had to run hard to fetch it; but it was too late and doubtful, in any case, whether it would have helped. She was buried in a little coffin in Stratton-on-the-Fosse churchyard. Mollie was shattered and I spent most of the next two days at home with her. Bridget must have gone straight to Heaven: we asked her to pray for us and within twenty-four hours came the news of the house loan from Westminster Cathedral.

In 1966 my father decided to retire. He had already resigned from his Archdeaconry but he was now 82 and very unsteady on his feet, so that he found great difficulty in walking from his vicarage to the church. He had been at Stanton Lacy for twelve years. I thought that, although they would have to leave their friends in Shropshire, it would be best for them to move down to Somerset where Mollie and I could keep an eye on them. I found them a house in Croscombe, called Dormans, which they re-christened Corvedale, to remind them of their previous haunts. Before they left Shropshire they had a sale of many of the contents of the vicarage. These included some extremely valuable furniture of my mother's, and other items of sentimental value, such as silhouettes of my father's family, dating from the 1830s. Mother never had any idea of the value of things and, instead of taking proper advice, entrusted everything to dealers. The result was price rings; the furniture was sold off dirt cheap; they raised enough money to pay for a few alterations and repairs to the new house but there was nothing left after that. Although they never had to sell their gold fillings, they had to live carefully and had they been forced to live on my father's pension, would have starved. Fortunately Mother still had some of her money. On the Sunday after their arrival at Corvedale they lay in bed, listening to the church bells; no more services, no more sermons, they thought. But they had forgotten that the habits of a lifetime are not easily broken: they had such qualms of conscience that they went to church the following Sunday and every Sunday after that until they grew too infirm. In 1967 they celebrated their golden wedding at our house and the family gave them a concert.

It was Mollie's and my turn to celebrate our Silver Wedding during the next year, 1968. A Mass, celebrated by Dom Cuthbert and sung by the children, was held in Downside Abbey and my father preached the sermon. This was followed by a party at Parsonage Farm. The children gave us a bag containing £50 in coins; this was an allusion to some feature in 'The Beano', details of which I can no longer remember.

In 1969 our last child, Benjamin, was born. I remember feeling superstitious because, visiting the boys at the Choir School with my mother, we took them to Madame Tussaud's. While waiting for them, I saw a machine which answered various questions if you pressed the buttons; one of these said 'How many children am I going to have?' Well, I thought to myself, they will hardly have the number of my children in the machine, so I will test it out; I put my sixpence in the slot and out came a card with the answer: Thirteen! I was dumbfounded and not a little uneasy, since Ben, who was on the way, would be number fourteen. However, I need not have worried, as all went well. Ben, being six years younger than his nearest brother, had a different sort of upbringing; he was like an only child and went about with us everywhere; we had no nannies or surrogate mothers. He was a very happy and placid child, so we had no difficulty. Later on he never went through the period of 'teenage-itis'; neither, for that matter, did most of the other children; but perhaps we never noticed.

The Seventies began with the death of my father in January. He had been declining for several years and was never disposed to leave his chair, even when he would have been able to do so. As a result of senile diabetes, gangrene set in. He did not appear to suffer pain. Two others close to us died during the next two years, Uncle Hughe and Fr. Beddoes. Uncle Hughe's sudden death appeared to affect my mother more than my father's. At the latter she had decided to carry on with her routine without deviation, even to the point of having Abbot Passmore to dinner the night after Father died. Uncle Hughe's death, however, upset her a great deal, although, naturally, she did not cry; but she did have an upset stomach for days.

The Family Choir drove to Newtown to sing at Fr. Beddoes' funeral: Bishop Petit sang the Mass (he died himself not long afterwards) and the interment took place a mile from the town. A huge procession, consisting, it seemed, of every inhabitant of Newtown, followed the coffin. They recognised in the end his true worth.

The Seventies were notable not only for deaths but also for weddings: Gwen was married in 1970 to Dr Timothy Williamson and my first grandchild, Rachel, was born the following year. Then in 1972 Mary was married to Michael Fysh, a barrister and an old boy of Downside, who had been a treble in my first choral society. John followed two years later; he was beginning to prosper in the antique book business, in which he is still engaged. He married Jennifer Wheeler.

The outstanding family activity during this decade was the Family Choir. During the Sixties we had given a few concerts either locally or near my parents in Shropshire. Shortly after Ben was born I took the choir to Germany, where we stayed with my friend from All Hallows, James Douglas. He was curate at Plettenberg in the Sauerland. We gave five or six concerts, compèred by James, but not very well attended. Before we started for home I bought a large tin of German sausages; it was heavy and a great trouble to handle. I had to run with it on the platform at Cologne and again up countless staircases on to the boat. A concerned stewardess invited me to sit down and rest, as I was puffing like a grampus. At Dover it was left on the platform, so that at Victoria I had to send the family home and wait for the tin to arrive by the next train. I carried it back to Croscombe and dumped it with relief in the kitchen. Next day I went shopping in Shepton Mallet and there, in the supermarket, was a tin exactly the same!

I took all the family to Bristol for a BBC audition. The result was a number of televised appearances on HTV at Bristol and Westward TV at Plymouth, culminating in a complete film entitled 'Harmony at Parsonage Farm' which was broadcast before Christmas 1976. The camera crew spent several days with us at different seasons of the year; this was the driest summer of the century and I had to be filmed digging the garden; all that came up on the spade was a cloud of dust and the vegetables were all dead. At this time we also began to sing in Downside Abbey for Christmas midnight Mass and the Holy Week ceremonies. In 1978 we sang at the Brompton Oratory in aid of the Downside Appeal. We had already made our first record 'Music in the Family' in 1975 and another 'Family Album', was to follow. The programmes were mainly Latin church music, folk songs and madrigals – not exactly popular music – and for this reason we never became a box office success nor 'Top of the Pops'. In 1978 we also went for our second foreign tour, beginning at Brussels and continuing in Holland at Rotterdam, Alkmaar and the Hook of Holland. Then on to Denmark to sing in various Lutheran Cathedrals, ending up, though not singing, at a famous nudist bathing beach which was full of Germans. Our organiser for all this was Gillie Cannon, from Bath. She managed many concerts for us and helped to put us on the road to fame. The question was whether we were going to develop our singing and become professionals. At one time, after two concerts at St John's, Smith Square, and a performance of Duruflés Requiem in Wells Cathedral, it looked as if this could happen. Understandably, however, many of the children were not keen. Those recently married were mothers of young children, others were at school or university and would have been ill advised to have interrupted their studies. A television crew arrived to hear us with a view to several weeks' work on Southern TV. They remarked that the choir did not seem to be very keen, so the idea was dropped. We gave a few concerts later on but gradually drifted into singing for weddings, which did not entail long and frequent rehearsals. Rather than prolong the image of 'Daddy and his children', with which they had grown up, I handed over the conducting to David and we had some successful concerts in the Eighties; rehearsal with the family now so far scattered is almost impossible.

My father and my mother used to go on holiday to Devonshire. Apart from eating large meals, their main occupation was to drive the car to some beauty spot and sit there reading their books. Mollie and I poured scorn on this at the time, but twenty years later we discovered that this was not a bad way of spending a holiday. After Father's death, Mother liked me to go on holiday with her to Hope Cove in South Devon. I drove her to the beauty spots and went for a walk, while she sat in the car. Mother could be very embarrassing. On one occasion there were several large dogs in the hotel; I am not a dog lover, but certainly did not object to their presence. The first evening we sat in the lounge and a giant mastiff approached; I preserved, I thought, a stiff upper lip and neither by look nor gesture betrayed my apprehension. 'Look out' cried Mother, 'Keep that dog away from my son; he *hates* dogs.' I felt like crawling underneath the nearest armchair. In Alderney, where we went in 1979, Mother ordered crab for dinner. The crab arrived sitting on her plate, no one having attempted to prepare it; it is all very well tackling a crab like that on the beach, but in the dining room of the Grand Hotel, it presented problems. I did what I could to prepare the dish for her assault, but no sooner had she started than claws and lumps of crab meat began sailing through the air onto the plates of the other diners. I had to drink a bottle of their superb claret before I recovered.

In the early 1980s I took Mother by air to Jersey. As we sat down to dinner, she peered hard at a looking-glass on the opposite wall, which reflected our two figures. 'Oh look!' she said. 'What a coincidence; there are the Archdeacon of Wells and his wife. Do go and say hello to them.' So I had to walk across the room and shake hands with my own reflection.

Although she was willing to visit the Channel Islands and to fly for the first time in her life when she was in her eighties, she would never go to a foreign country. Many years earlier she had been persuaded and reluctantly agreed to go on a day trip to Boulogne, or 'Bolone' as she called it. The day was a disaster; she told me that the French must be fools because when she asked the way to the 'Bois de Boulogne', no one could tell her. To add insult to injury someone, obviously a Frenchman, was sick all over her on the boat coming back.

Foreign holidays for Mollie and me did not start until 1976, when

Mary invited us to spend ten days in Brittany with her. We did this for five years running, staying at different places and twice at Audierne. I was amazed to see how well the French lived; at the enormous variety of fish which they devoured and the skill with which they cooked them. It is depressing to think that the same fish swim in our own waters, and that most of the prawns they eat in France are sucked by hoovers from the Scottish lochs. But then the English are not interested in food; they think there is something faintly disgusting in paying any attention to it. Uncle Hughe once took my father out to dinner at the Savoy; he ordered fish and chips. Mother was furious.

In the early 1980s Michael and Mary bought a beautiful house in the Dordogne, near Verteillac; there was a swimming pool in the garden. Mollie and I stayed with them there every year and I was able to visit the vineyards of Bordeaux and Bergerac, which were within easy reach. I even learnt how to make *foie gras*.

# CHAPTER XVI

# Death in the Family

In 1985 Lady Becket, a local musical magnate, asked me to tea and over the rock buns invited me to take charge of a choir she had collected, to sing for a harvest festival at Hornblotton. I agreed and the result was the St Dunstan Singers. We sang for the harvest festival and it was Lady Becket's hope that we should go round the local villages, helping out whenever we were needed. There were two difficulties over this: first, I was a Catholic and while not objecting to Evensong, weddings or funerals, I drew the line at Communion services; secondly, not many vicars seemed to be crying out for our assistance. We therefore, without ruling out services, decided to focus our energies on concerts. We have given two concerts each year since then and the choir, although small and of advanced average age, seems to be flourishing.

At approximately the same time I was asked to play the organ at the eleven o'clock Mass at St John's, Bath. My duties also extended to weddings. St John's, built in 1862 by the Downside monks, is one of the finest examples of neo-gothic architecture. Staffed by monks until the mid-1930s, it was eventually handed over to the Bishop; the Parish Priest in 1985 was Canon James Kelly. The chief reason for my appointment was my ability to accompany the Chant, of which there had been a long tradition at St John's. The organ was in bad repair, having been built on the cheap after the blitz; when I arrived it had not been tuned, it seemed, for over a year. The music was under the direction of David and Elizabeth Bates, both children of Cuthbert Bates, ex-director of the Tudor Singers and of the Bath Bach Choir. Cuthbert had been succeeded by his son, Richard, who died suddenly and tragically in 1985 and it was because of this that I was asked to come and play.

It was wonderful to be involved with the Chant again. We sang it all the time at Newtown and for part of the time at All Hallows before the

changes. At Downside it had almost disappeared when they began to
sing the Office in English. After Canon Kelly's retirement from St John's
his successor tried hard to replace the Chant by modern music, but did
not succeed. The preservation of high standards of church music
demands constant watchfulness and not a few battles.

This new work effectively filled up my time during retirement and it
was not long before I was as busy as I had been while in full
employment.

Accounts of happy marriages can be supremely uninteresting to the
reader, unless he is himself involved. Such is the fallen state of man that
fornication, adultery, lust and murder are infinitely more absorbing. I
must, however, ask the reader to bear with me while I recount the
family weddings of the 1980s.

During this decade eight of our children were married. Rachel was
the first to go and in the spring of 1981 she married John Carter, son of
Dr Carter, who had seen many of our children into the world. In the
same year Stella married Howard Arman; the wedding took place at
Stratton-on-the-Fosse. Stella and I were driving the eight miles to the
church when she suddenly cried out 'I've left my bouquet behind'. We
had to turn round and fetch it, eventually arriving half-an-hour late.
The guests all thought that Stella had changed her mind; only one
person was pleased: Joe, the best man, had lost the marriage licence and
needed the time to look for it; he finally found it in the waste paper
basket in the Sacristy. After the marriage Stella and Howard went to
live first at Munich and later at Innsbruck where they began to make
their names in the musical world. In 1983 David married Clare Bowler-
Reed at the Holy Redeemer Church, Chelsea, where David was in
charge of the music. Very sadly, after ten years of married life, crowned
by the birth of five beautiful children, the marriage broke down and
they separated. This tragedy cast a cloud over the first half of the 1990s
for the whole family. Joe, in the same year, married Clare Smithies, the
doctor-daughter of Judge Kenneth Smithies, whose son I taught at
Downside. They have at present six children and no doubt the number
will increase. I seem to have inherited the promise made to Abraham
that his descendants should be as the sand on the seashore: at the time
of writing I have 37 grandchildren. Helen was married in 1984 at
Shepton Mallet to James Ross. Fr. James Douglas came over from
Germany to conduct the ceremony; Helen tells me that as I led her into
the church I said to her 'Behave yourself and stop grinning at your
friends; try to look dignified.' She admits that this final exercise of
paternal authority did some good to her nerves!

Tony's wedding, also at Shepton Mallet, was the first local one in the family. His bride, Alice Lippett, had been born and bred in Croscombe and her family had been known to us ever since our arrival. Much of the ceremony, however, passed me by, since I was suffering from such a bad attack of sciatica that I had to spend the morning lying flat on the floor and found the seat in church excruciatingly painful. Rupert followed in 1988, another Holy Redeemer wedding this time, to Sarah Owen, who had been a member of David's choir. They went to live in Bath where Rupert at that time ran a gardening business. He later gained a B.Sc. degree and trained as a teacher. Daniel's was the last wedding, also at the Holy Redeemer, in 1989, to Clancy Brett, whom he had met in London while carrying out his financial dealings in the City. They are both very keen on hunting and spend weekends at their cottage in the Cotswolds. I have only three children who are unmarried, Jeremy, Cicely and Ben, a situation which will doubtless be remedied before long. That is unless one of them has a vocation for the religious life. I have always hoped that one of my children would become a priest or a nun, but time is now running out.

After Father's death, Mother stayed alone at Corvedale, still active in her early eighties. She had played a leading part with Mollie in founding the weekly village market, held on Tuesdays, and contributed a constant supply of home-made meringues and marmalade. Her eightieth birthday had been celebrated in 1973 with a party of all her friends at Parsonage Farm. On this occasion I made a speech which is included at the end of this book. She remained active for another ten years, but during that time began to suffer from arthritis of the hip. Nothing daunted, she went into hospital for a hip replacement and just before she returned home, announced to me 'In future I'm only going to do the things I want to do, so don't try to make me do anything different.'

There was another party in Dinder Parish hall for her ninetieth birthday. For this Countess Mountbatten, who was married to Lord Brabourne, the head of Mother's family, came from Kent. Mother was in a wheelchair, but very much alert. We sang her a Birthday Ode set to music culled from her favourite church anthems and canticles.

She had walked quite easily for a time but slowly her knees began to be affected by the arthritis. She resorted to a 'zimmer' frame, but soon began to fall over in the house. It was time to do something. Mollie helped as much as she could, but her own disease was developing and she eventually found it impossible to walk down to Corvedale. I took over Mother's evening meal, while she had, much to her disgust, 'Meals on Wheels' at midday. In 1984 they took her into the local hospital at Shepton Mallet, where she was happy, as soon as she had grown used to it, but never very sociable. She could not easily adjust herself to the other patients: 'They're all crackers' she remarked. She found the daily activities, if you could call them that, excruciatingly boring: the patients sat in two groups, men at one end watching television, women at the other watching two canaries copulating in a cage.

The doctors could find nothing wrong with Mother except old age and declared that she must move into a nursing home. Mollie and I wanted her to go back to Corvedale, but it would have been impossible with me at work and Mollie infirm, so she went to a nursing home in Glastonbury. I used to drive out three or four times a week to see her and occasionally Mollie was able to accompany me. She made several attempts at dying: on one occasion she seemed about to slip away and the nurses were just going to telephone me, when Mother suddenly sat up in bed and said: 'Well, I think a cup of tea would be in order.' A few days later she really did die, at three o'clock in the morning. When I went to the nursing home the night before with Mollie's brother, Rupert, the whole town was seething with crowds preparing for the Carnival. We had to have a police escort to take us to the home. She was buried with my father at Dinder, the small village where my parents used to go to church.

In the mid-1970s Mollie noticed some slight difficulty in climbing stairs; her legs ached and seemed to lose power. At first the doctor said that he was not surprised, seeing all the work she was doing. Over the next year or two, however, things got worse and she suffered from aching legs for much of the time. Finally in 1981 the doctor diagnosed Polymyositis, a disease very rare, but resembling multiple sclerosis in its symptoms. Just before she began treatment we went with Ben to stay in Germany with our friends Wilfrid and Lutzi Köhler. Mollie seemed better for a while and even managed a five mile walk in the hills and woods. In September, however, she was very tired after the preparations for Stella's wedding and a few days later was admitted to the Royal Mineral Water Hospital in Bath. There they gave her innumerable tests until they found the right drug. It was during the long hours of waiting there that she began to write her autobiography *Against All Advice*. It was a hard task putting it together, because Mollie's habit was to write extremely illegibly (only I could read her writing) on odd sheets of paper, often deviating on to a new subject before she had finished with the old one. We managed between us, however, to piece together a very readable book, which we published ourselves before Christmas. It sold about 1,500 copies.

Mollie's drug had to be administered weekly by a doctor, which sometimes caused difficulties. The following August we went as usual to stay with Mary in the Dordogne. I had to get the local doctor to give the injection but puzzled her somewhat when, forgetting the French for muscles, I said 'Elle a mal aux moules!' I think the doctor thought she had been overeating.

Eventually the drug began to cause nausea and the doctors wanted her to return to hospital to have her liver examined. Mollie would have none of that; she would rather die, she said, then have any more treatment. For a few weeks she had no drugs but her condition began to worsen so quickly that she had to take steroids, the only known alternative to what she had previously taken. Soon she could no longer walk without the aid of a frame on wheels and was spending most of her time in a chair.

At this time we decided that Parsonage Farm needed much repair work and we also wanted a conservatory where Mollie could sit instead of being cooped up indoors. The children generously clubbed together to pay the interest on a £20,000 loan, which enabled the work to be done. The conservatory was just what Mollie needed and she spent most of her time there except in the depth of winter. We continued our reading together as we had done for the past forty years. We were both looking forward to our golden wedding in February 1993, for which Paul Ketterer had generously offered us the use of the school chapel and catering staff at All Hallows.

Mollie grew slowly weaker; she was not in pain, but obviously frustrated. Having been so active throughout her life, it irked her to be confined to a chair. In order to avoid stairs, which she could not now climb, we had a hand-operated lift constructed to take her to her bedroom. It would have been wiser to have moved the bedroom downstairs, because after about two years Mollie had to have an automatic wheelchair and the lift had to go. She had already fallen backwards out of it when attempting to hold on to her trolley before ascending.

Although she was so infirm, she was otherwise in very good health and able to enter into every activity, whether it was plucking hens or geese or cutting up a pig. We still kept sheep, pigs, geese and hens on the farm; the goats had gone by now. Gradually, however, Mollie's arms grew weaker, first her left, then her right. Finally John constructed a crane which he attached to her right wrist, fixing a counter-weight at the back of the chair which enabled her to raise and lower her arm. She could always feed herself, but swallowing was becoming difficult and it was this which in the end caused her death.

During her closing years Mollie would often say 'When I am better, I will do so and so'. She nevertheless managed to cram a good deal of activity into this time, even the embroidery of a giant tapestry which now hangs in my room. She knew that she was slowly dying and devoted much of her day to prayer and meditation, sitting for hours in the little oratory we had made for her. With the money Mother had left me I bought a van especially built to hold a wheelchair. She could propel herself into the back and we could drive anywhere. Two days before she died I drove her to Mass in Shepton Mallet.

During September 1992 we had disturbing news that the village market, which Mollie had founded in the late Sixties, was to be closed. Meddlesome officials had threatened to inspect the kitchens of all who cooked food for sale. My letter to the Daily Telegraph aroused some interest and a photographer came down; our picture, the last ever taken of Mollie, appeared in the paper. Mollie, however, was very upset over the affair.

By the end of October she could hardly swallow and the district nurse gave her morphine to counteract the discomfort; she still had no pain. On the morning of 23rd October Mollie woke up and said to me 'Today is the day. Send for Father Lessiter' (her spiritual director). He drove down from the Midlands, heard her confession and gave her the Last Sacraments. Meanwhile I had sent for the children and nearly all of them came. She talked with some of them in the morning and in the afternoon I read to her for the last time.

At 11 pm she was still talking with us in the sitting room when the nurse arrived to take her to bed. 'Good night' she said 'don't forget to put your watches back.' She drove herself down the passage. After about fifteen minutes we heard the nurse call and rushed to the bedroom. The nurse told us what had happened: Mollie had washed herself, prepared for bed and had put on the harness which attached her to an overhead rail, via which she was normally conveyed to the bedroom. All the time she was smiling, something which her paralysed mouth normally prevented her from doing; she seemed to be recognising someone and saying 'St Peter.' Then she died. The nurse, who was a Methodist, told us that she had seen hundreds of people die, but never like this. It made, she said, a tremendous impression on her. When I approached the bed, Mollie was already cold. She was buried next to my parents at Dinder, opposite the house where Rachel lived and it is to that place that I shall eventually follow her.

There was standing room only in the little church at Shepton Mallet. The boys sang the Requiem in plainchant and Rachel sang *In Paradisum*. We had the Old Mass.

# CHAPTER XVII

## *Retirement*

Throughout our married life Mollie and I had been very close. When, a few years before her death, that event presented itself as likely to happen in the foreseeable future. I shrank at the thought. I did not see how I could survive the separation. In the event, however, a curious thing happened: I was able to accept it with something like equanimity and managed to continue with my daily life and work almost as if it had not been interrupted. I ascribe this to Mollie's prayers. Her life, especially near the end, had been exemplary; Fr. Lessiter, himself a man of God, was certain that she was in Heaven, and I do not think that he said so merely to console me. She is in Heaven, praying for us all.

The immediate problem was what to do with the house; it would have been impracticable for me to have stayed alone in a big, rambling farmhouse. Mollie and I had both decided to offer it rent free to David and his family. They had recently moved to Croscombe and David was working at Prior Park College, Bath, going up to Chelsea at weekends for his work at the Holy Redeemer Church. He had already bought a house in Croscombe, but it was too small for a wife and five children. I persuaded him and Clare to let it and move into Parsonage Farm. I retained for myself a flat, which was adapted so as to give me a sitting room, bathroom, kitchen, bedroom and conservatory, ample, even luxurious for a single person.

I should have remembered that a large family was a powerful force; Clare was surrounded by rooms and furniture which reminded her of someone else and had the feeling of not being mistress of her own domain. She was clearly unhappy. But this did not prepare us for the blow which struck after less than a year, when she left David, taking the children with her to Berkshire. David was prostrated and has never recovered from the disaster. He moved back into his cottage in the village and I was alone.

For the first three months after Mollie's death, while building operations were in progress in my flat, I had moved into Rachel and John Carter's house in Dinder. Shortly after Clare's departure they had to sell the Dinder house and were looking for less expensive accommodation. They wanted to move to Parsonage Farm, but wisely decided that if this idea was to be successful, they must own the property. Accordingly they bought it from me, allowing me to live on in my flat. They completely reorganised both house and garden. Although I missed the familiar rooms and furniture, there is no doubt that they improved the property immensely. With my teaching programme drastically reduced, I prepared myself for the final period of my life, during which, to use Roscoe Beddoes' phrase, I should strive to become 'holy and learned'. I doubt whether I shall achieve either, but it is a pleasant thought.

Looking back on my past life I wonder which events influenced it most. My change of religion probably had the most far-reaching effect, for it altered my career. But for my conversion, I might have ended as a country vicar, not the Trollopian type living in a spacious rectory amid idyllic scenes of rural bliss, but a member of countless committees with six parishes to serve. Had I not quitted the Church of England when I did, I am sure that I should not have remained in it to survive the new order of service nor women priests. Becoming a Catholic not only changed my career but gradually promoted a new outlook on life and some realisation of what it was all about. At the same time I have preserved from my Anglican days a firm belief in the importance of divine worship, that it should be conducted with as much dignity and ceremony as possible; we all know that the early Christians worshipped without the paraphernalia of later centuries, but then they were a persecuted minority. The Church is a living organism, which reacts to social change and adapts itself to circumstances, without altering its essential teaching. The office of Bishop is an exalted one; however unworthy the man, his office demands a respect which the pre-Vatican II Church showed by elaborate dress and ceremonial. Much of this has been abolished as 'triumphalism'. I have seen bishops walking about dressed as junior curates, or hiding their pectoral crosses in a waistcoat pocket, as if to say 'I am really no better than you'. We all know that. The priests are worse: they add words to the Mass, of which the least appropriate is 'Good morning everybody'. Is not 'The grace of Our Lord Jesus Christ ...' more suited to the impersonal nature of the liturgy?

The new sin of triumphalism has caused a further casualty: the pulpit. Originally constructed to enable the preacher to be both visible and audible, this useful piece of furniture has been relegated to limbo or the storage of mops and buckets. So neglected has become the art of elocution that few preachers can be heard speaking from the altar steps, unless they use a Tannoy system. This is often unreliable. I have not heard a sermon in Bath for five years.

It has been my privilege to spend most of my life teaching; this is what I have enjoyed most. I am not a musician in the truest sense of the word: my performing abilities are limited and I seldom go to concerts; I do not even like talking about music and feel somewhat irritated when people whom I meet feel that a musical conversation is appropriate. I do not pretend that this is a virtue and am sure that if I attended more concerts I should be a better musician. My egocentricity is such that I only enjoy music to the full when I am taking part or conducting it myself.

Another interest which has occupied both Mollie and me has been self-sufficiency. Our large family forced us to plan our economy so that we produced as much as possible without being dependent on shops. In our excursions into English literature we soon discovered the works of Cobbett who became our guide and philosopher. We learnt much from his *Cottage Economy*. At Downside Lodge, where we had no land of our own, we managed to borrow two fields on which to graze our cow. The first, Flicker, was an Aberdeen Angus, really a beef breed, but she gave us enough milk; when she died of a rare disease, her successor, a Guernsey named Hope, provided enough for us to churn our own butter; the sight of a golden mound of this revived our spirits every morning at breakfast time. We kept a goat at the same time, grazing it on the lawn, and Mollie used its milk to make cheese. We kept two pigs at a time, fattening them on scraps from the table mixed with pig meal. Mr Gay, a licensed slaughterer from Radstock, used to come over and neatly dispatch the animals, after which the larder simply groaned with food. Nothing was wasted; Mollie made brawn or sausages from the heads, laboriously stuffing in the meat by hand. We kept hens, of course, and even attempted rabbits. These, however, unusually for their kind, and perhaps out of jealousy of their owners, refused to breed. Once at Croscombe, with two acres of our own, we replaced the cow with a flock of sheep. I had an unfortunate experience with our first lambs; I took them to a slaughterhouse and was told to come back next day to collect the carcasses. When I did so, they could not be found; the carcasses with which I was presented were clearly old mutton and had

'Radstock Co-op' stamped on them. I learnt my lesson and in future asked a farmer friend, whom the slaughterers knew, to take the lambs.

We were tolerably well supplied with meat. Fish was a different matter. We had two fish ponds dug in our field and stocked them with gudgeon, roach and suchlike — even crayfish. Unfortunately, herons flew straight over from the moors and breakfasted daily on our fish; a few small crayfish were all that we ever harvested.

We grew our vegetables, of course; potatoes usually lasted until November but we had greens all through the year. In spite of this we still had to shop for some things. For several months I tried the local shops, but none of these were able to give us reduced terms for large quantities. Luckily, Messrs L. & F. Jones, with whom we had traded in a small way when they owned a shop in Stratton-on-the-Fosse during the late Sixties, opened a wholesale 'Cash and Carry' at Radstock and generously gave me an admission card. Henceforth I could buy wholesale and in bulk; L. & F. Jones came to my rescue when my dependants were at their most numerous and the family economy most perilous.

# *Epilogue*

Father Wilfrid Passmore once told me that I should never regret having a large family. In the early days I should be oppressed by poverty, hard work and anxiety. Later on, however, we should have our reward. I only half believed him at the time, as I saw before me a never-ending stretch of bills, overdrafts, school reports and wet nappies. He was right, however. Now that I have reached old age I am not likely to be lonely. I am visited constantly by the family, am taken by them for expensive holidays abroad and showered with presents. It is almost overwhelming.

Looking back, I can see that I have been a very fortunate man: I was brought up in a happy home, received an expensive education, survived the war without a scratch, married the most wonderful wife; my work has always been interesting and congenial; nearly all my children still practise their religion and shower me with love and constant attention. I have done nothing to deserve this, indeed according to fashionable modes of thought, by having so many children I have recklessly courted disaster. Yet, when disaster has seemed imminent, I have always been saved.

Let King David have the last word:

> Lo, children and the fruit of the womb are an heritage and gift that cometh of the Lord. Like as the arrows in the hand of the giant, even so are the young children. Happy is the man that hath his quiver full of them.
>
> *Psalm 127*

# *Appendix*

## SPEECH GIVEN ON MY MOTHER'S EIGHTIETH
## BIRTHDAY

There is no need for me to remind you of the great anniversary which we are celebrating today. No one who has known my mother for any length of time could ever have doubted that, God willing, she would reach her eightieth birthday in full command of her powers, still exercising that personality which we have all learnt to cherish and respect. Her life has been full and eventful and has continued so even in her retirement.

What some of you may not realise is that of those eighty years at least two have been spent — day and night, 24 hours each day — in church. It is true that on their retirement my parents decided that they would take a holiday from Church attendance. All was well on the first Sunday; the Croscombe bells rang out, but from Corvedale only snores were heard. The second Sunday saw my mother idly thumbing the pages of the hymn book, 'I wonder that they are having today' she asked. On the third Sunday it was *Harwood in A flat* and *Blessed be the God and Father* at the Cathedral. Enough, resolutions were flung to the winds and they became living examples of the scriptural precept 'the zeal of thy house hath eaten me up'.

Of course, a lifetime of church services has had, among others, one important effect — it has made my mother an authority, the greatest in England — the world — who knows? — on hymns, and it is fitting, therefore, to present her with the following eightieth birthday tribute, which comes with the compliments of the editors of *Hymns Ancient and Modern* (unrevised):—

Hymn No 299 *Come let us join our cheerful songs*; (651) *Glory to God the Morn appointed breaks*. If all her sons could have been here and Christopher could have been brought (358) *From Greenland's icy mountains, from India's coral strand* we could have seen (679) *Brothers going hand in hand*, in fact (729) *As now Thy children lowly kneel*, we should be the first to say (450) *Shall we not love thee mother dear?*, and (457) *How blest the matron who endured* (290) *Through all the changing scenes of life*, although naturally, (174) *We saw Thee not when Thou didst come*.

No doubt to many of us who reach the age of eighty a voice may sometimes whisper (254) *Art Thou weary?* and suggest that because (19)

*The radiant morn hath passed away,* therefore, (135) *The strife is o'er.* But mother has never listened to that voice — if in fact it has ever spoken to her. Her motto has always been (738) *Come labour on* and (269) *Christian seek not yet repose,* because (288) *A few more years shall roll.* To conclude, however, it is not only a matter of (545) *Glorious things of thee are spoken,* but we welcome all our friends and relations who have come to congratulate her with (153) *Joyse, because the circling year brings our day of blessings here.* And to you all we say thank you for coming and (740) *God be with you till we meet again.*

So, let us raise our glasses and in the words of our final hymn — which comes, not from A & M, but from a more trendy volume 'Teenage Ditties for Croscombe Youth' (with apologies to the Rector)

> We lift our glass to you O Joyse
> And sing to you with heart and voise